The Colony

The Colony

JOHN BOWERS

E. P. DUTTON & CO., INC. | NEW YORK | 1971

Published simultaneously in Canada by Clarke, Irwin &
Company Limited, Toronto and Vancouver

Library of Congress Catalog Card Number: 77-133598
SBN 0-525-08270-0

Part One

A narrow, graveled road led into the Colony. A printed sign at the entrance warned that trespassing was absolutely forbidden. But I had written to Lowney Handy, been told I didn't have the makings of a writer, had written again in a testy way, been accepted, and now drove through the gate in a green, 1951 Cambridge Plymouth, which I had proudly come by after graduating from college.

I had left a town in East Tennessee, a place of twenty-eight thousand, where the Southern Railway slices exactly through its geographical heart. As a child I had tightrope-walked down its tracks, carrying my father's supper to him

3

in a tin container that had once held a Christmas fruitcake. My father worked as a telegrapher at the depot, a tall, silent-moving man. Forty-two would come screaming through, and he would stand nearer to it than anyone, holding up the bamboo hoop with messages for the high-perched engineer to snag. He never missed a day of work. Through sickness and anger, through World Series and World Wars, he did not miss one day of duty. Ever. And he never had a kind word to say for it. It took the whole country's economy, the Depression, to slow him, causing him to endure temporary railroad jobs in smaller, more desolate Southern towns, leaving family behind. What a man had to do, he did.

And he stayed with one woman, my mother. He thought so much of her—with a tinge of fear, too, perhaps—that he kept the Four Roses and Gilbey-gin pints hidden in the coal bin and would never take a pull on one in front of her. He never swore in front of her—except when cataclysmically provoked from the outside. (He once stood in her presence and shouted an expletive at Raymond Graham Swing when the "announcement of worldwide importance" turned out to be a pitch for a laxative.)

My mother, bright-eyed and cheerful, would admit she was a bit of a Puritan. As an ex-schoolteacher she knew her definitions; she had worn out several dictionaries. But Puritan or not, East Tennessean or not, she tried to understand the outside and bring the knowledge home. The Sunday *New York Times* was wedged into the wire loop of the mailbox on Monday. She took me by train and by hand to Knoxville to hear Josef Hofmann play the piano and Carl Sandburg the guitar. When I was so small my legs couldn't touch the floor in a straight-back chair, she took me to hear a world-famous journalist speak at a banquet. ("If I have learned one thing

4

from my travels to the Far East," he said, a year before Pearl Harbor, "it is that there will be no war. What do we want with a burned-out island?") Our home might be the last to own a TV set, a radio, a car—but books grew from floor to ceiling, new shelves going up every few years. My father would stretch out on the couch, reading Dickens, my mother leafing through the essays of Mark Twain; everything safe and secure and cozy. At odd hours, though, my father would rise and trudge down to the depot.

And—visiting him, carrying his supper—I watched the warmly lit windows of those trains going by. From the dining cars, finely dressed people looked out boredly, seeming to hold all the world's secrets, faces unlike any that you met up and down Market Street. The trains, though, were a backdrop for the Town. The Town was what mattered. When I began to lust after girls, I had to shy away for the longest time because our family owned no car, the only arena for courtship, a spaceship to the drive-in or woods. (Crazed at seventeen with the need for a car once, I borrowed one without knowing how to shift gears, drove jerkily in first and second to a drive-in movie, and crashed, with my arm around a terror-stricken girl, into a pole.) Meeting the Town's leading citizens, often as not in pursuit of their daughters, I was shamed when they had no knowledge of my father. For although the Town was all I could remember, my family had moved to it from another town down the railroad line when I was a baby, not really having roots in it themselves. Other people in Tennessee hadn't followed the rails the way we had; most dated back in the Town several generations. So many lived in fine homes, the fathers earning a livelihood in the standard professions. A half-Greek and a boy whose father had abandoned home were my fondest friends. My

5

older, curly-haired brother had lettered in five sports, a star athlete. He had shown the world, and I must too. And I knew I could up the road. *Life* (the magazine) said I could, and at twenty-three I believed, like Candide, what I heard and read.

*

I first saw a low-slung building that had screens around the sides and picnic benches set up at one end for dining. There was a long, narrow building that contained a series of rooms, like a miniature motel, all with desks, typewriters, and cots. There were trees, stretches of mowed lawn with a water spigot or two jutting up, and brick paths. A silverish trailer was there—like the one *Life* magazine reported that James Jones lived in—with a smaller, red and yellow one nearby. There were some army tents, a squarish prefab that looked like a guesthouse, and a small white frame building that looked like nothing else in the place. It was all eerily quiet, because there was not one soul there when I drove in that summer afternoon in 1952.

"Hey, anybody home?" I yelled. How strange my voice sounded.

At the silverish trailer I peeked through the screen door and saw a typewriter with manuscript-looking paper to either side and an unabridged Webster's close at hand. I hoped that perhaps somewhere near the door would be a discarded manuscript page so that for the first time in my life I could see what a famous novelist's workings looked like in the raw. Just think, here I stand where James Jones wrote parts of *From Here to Eternity*. No matter how hard I strained my eyes I couldn't make out what was written on the sheets by

6

the typewriter, and I was afraid of entering the trailer. Afraid of being caught. I peered into the tiny rooms in the motel-like structure, but could tell little about the occupants—whoever they might be. There were no pictures or paintings or personal souvenirs. Really Spartan. The clothing, which was neatly stored, looked like Army Surplus and backwoodsmen's outfits. Boy, everybody a real writer! None of those boring, narrow-minded Republicans I was used to in my hometown. I lay back against a tall shade tree, where I had a view of the entrance, and went to sleep with a cool breeze blowing.

What awoke me was a young man, who appeared a few years younger than I, entering the compound. He was slight, already had a receding hairline, and over one eye a purplish bruise stood out. He must have been struck there not many hours before. He smiled, displaying loose upper bridgework. He was still in his teens. "Hi, I'm George." (His last name sounded like "Shab-butt," a name I'd never heard before; people back home had names like Smith and Rogers, mostly old English ones. His voice was very soft, his manner gentle.)

I told him who I was, and that I was joining the Colony. "I drove up from Tennessee," I said. "Say, where is everybody?"

"Oh," he said softly, "Mary Ann died last night. They found her this morning on the floor of her trailer. She died in a convulsion. Everybody got out of the Colony today and went to Terre Haute. Lowney and Jim and everybody. I got in a fight in a bar, and Lowney sent me back. I hope this don't develop into a bad black eye."

"It's probably going to be all right." But black eyes weren't on my mind. "Mary Ann? Was she a writer?"

7

"Yes," he said. "She was Jim's sister. She'd almost finished her book too, I think."

We ambled into the low, screened-in building, which he called the *ramada,* and he played host by fixing us both cups of coffee. "Lowney doesn't like for us to have coffee in the afternoons," he said shyly, "so I guess you better not tell her." Then, blowing into a hot mug of Instant Maxwell House: "Look, I'll give you fifty dollars if you can spell my last name."

"Do I have to bet anything myself?"

"No"—with that shy, funny smile—"go ahead."

"Say it for me once more."

It again sounded like "Shab-butt" but my mind wasn't on his name. I spelled something, a politician's smile on my face. After all, he was a member of the Colony and knew James Jones; I had just arrived.

"No," he said, "but you came fairly close. It starts with a 'T,' and no one knows to put it there." He wrote it down, and I looked at it, shaking my head and smiling more than I felt like doing. It looked unpronounceable. "It's an Indian name. My mother raised me on her own, and I'm not sure whose name it is. She's a waitress in Ohio. I'm seventeen, the youngest guy here."

I told him about an office job I had just left in Tennessee, about graduating from a university the year before ("You went to college?"), and about a girl friend I had left behind. We talked easily, plunging more freely into subjects and past taboos than I ever had with people in Tennessee. Back in Tennessee I had never run across anyone who was consumed with the madness to write.

"My stuff so far is all going to have to be burned," George said. "It's too much like Faulkner, and I've never been South.

8

That's what Lowney tells me. I've got to write about what I know."

"Does Jones live the way everyone else does at the Colony?"

"Pretty much so."

"You mean he sits down at that table and eats a meal just like everyone else?"

"Well, he has a martini with his meals. Lowney lets him."

"Is he like the characters in his book?"

"He's something like Prewitt, I think."

I asked when the others might come rolling into the Colony, and he was vague. Lowney might bring them in in a few minutes, or it could be late that night. I had not eaten for some time, and told him so.

"You'd better go on into Marshall and eat in a restaurant then. I doubt if Lowney will cook tonight. Mary Ann dying and all."

"Come with me. I'll set you up to a meal."

"No, I'd better stay here. Lowney told me not to leave."

I drove into town without fear, ate a meal with a couple of beers on the side, and then drove back to the Colony as dusk was settling. It was the restaurant meal a recruit eats just prior to going off to Basic Training.

*

As I wheeled the 1951 Plymouth back over the Colony's gray gravel, I saw that people were now moving around the compound and felt that others were there I couldn't see. A short stocky grandfather-type man, with sparse silver hair, loomed up in sports attire. That must be Lowney's husband. Should I say "Mister" to him, as I had done to all full-fledged adults in

9

Tennessee, or call him by his first name? "Hello. I just drove up from Tennessee," I said, pumping his hand, postponing the decision. Now I had to ask about his wife. Should it be "Lowney" or "Mrs. Handy"? What came out was, "Is Lowney around?"

"She's over at the *ramada*," he said jovially, a slur in his voice. "Just park your car and go in there. Welcome to the Colony."

"Thanks, Harry."

She was striding out of the *ramada* as I was walking up. Her tanned skin was coffee-colored, there were strands of gray through her black hair, and her eyes were huge. Her arms were short for her torso, thickish around the upper arms, and—lo and behold—she wore no brassiere. Her large breasts jumped—the only word for it—inside a sweat shirt, and I saw, with a catch in my throat, the outline of nipples. God, this had never happened in Tennessee! I kept my eyes raised, not wanting her to think I was interested in such things.

"Oh, hello there," she said in the warmest, kindest voice I have ever heard. "You must be my new boy from Tennessee. You know I'm from Kentucky, don't you? We could be related."

"It's real good to be here."

"I guess you heard we had a death here. Jim's sister, Mary Ann. Now Jim's getting ready to drive down to Peoria to see his brother, Jeff. Why don't you go over and say hello first. Oh, Jamie!"

I had read *From Here to Eternity* the year before. Lying on the sun roof of the ATO house in Knoxville, Tennessee, I had been Prewitt fighting the System, had played poker against the Warden, slugged it out with Bloom, and had gone on a

10

pass into Honolulu with Maggio. It was a book that had made me feel like a man, and in a way had made me thereafter see everything in a slightly different light—like being in love. It had never occurred to me that before going to college I had served a short stretch in the Army myself, in pre-war Korea with whores on straw mats and guard duty at thirty degrees below. It did not occur to me that it was exciting or romantic or worthy of recording simply because it had happened to me.

Now a man stood near a Chrysler convertible with tan leather seats. A wide-brim hat lay flat on his head, his shoes were brown and white wing tips, and there were suspenders under his wide-shouldered, wide-lapelled jacket. It was James Jones. He was shorter than I had imagined, but there was that rocklike jaw I had seen on the back of a book jacket. His eyes were greenish blue and looked right into you.

"Good to have you here," he said in a twang. His hand-shake was firm and quick, and close up I noticed that he had a neatly trimmed mustache. "Are you getting settled all right?"

"Yeah, everything's going O.K. . . . " I fumbled, jerked about, blushed a little. He was a Celebrity.

"Jamie, stop for the night if you get tired on the road," Lowney called, as he was driving off in his convertible.

"Aw, I'll be all right."

That evening a blur of faces passed by as I sat on the cold and smooth concrete steps in front of the *ramada* and waited to be given a room. Bayard, a wiry youth with a broken nose that slanted to the side, placed a bare foot on the concrete and talked to Lowney. She sat near me, the new arrival, rock-ing and hugging her legs against the June night air. Light-ning bugs pinpointed the darkness, and cricket sounds made

11

us know it was the country. They talked about things that made me feel more the stranger, made me want to belong more.

"That George is a pathological liar," Bayard said. "I don't believe some guy suddenly hit him in a bar for no reason. He just picked a hell of a time to cause trouble. How would it look in the papers? Colony member gets beaten up the day Jim's sister dies. We're just lucky he didn't get thrown in the pokey. It wouldn't break my heart if you kicked his ass out, Lowney."

"I don't know, I don't know," she said ladylike, rocking, dabbing a tear away. "Sometimes I think I'll just close this place and go off and work on my own book. I got a hell of a book in me."

"No, Lowney, you don't want to close the Colony."

"You should have seen what George turned in to me yesterday," she went on. "It opened with this family sitting around in a *log cabin*. They were eating *possum*, I'm not kidding you. I damn near threw up. When is he going to learn? Is he hopeless?"

I had no idea at all what I was going to write about. I reminded myself not to write about people in a log cabin eating possum.

"Don't you want to leave now?" she said to me, smiling, dabbing her eyes. "Before it's too late?"

"No, I'm glad I'm here. Boy, it's great to be out of that office I was in."

"This boy's from Tennessee, Bayard. Where can we put him tonight?"

I wanted to say that the roomy prefab in front of us seemed unoccupied, but Bayard said, "Let's stick him in a tent."

12

He led the way over a brick walk with a flashlight. "You sound as if you might be from the South yourself," I said, wanting to be friends with a Colony regular.

"You think so? Other people have told me that too. I've lived all my life right here in Illinois."

"Did you know Jones before he wrote *From Here to Eternity?*"

"Oh, yeah, I'd seen him around before he met Lowney. But he's older than me, so we were never buddies back then. I never really started off wanting to be a writer, you know. It happened after I got to know Lowney. How about you? What were you up to before this?"

"I was prostituting myself in a middle-class job," I said, and he laughed. Were we now friends?

An electric cord from somewhere stretched to the tent, and a naked hundred-watt bulb hung down in the center. The tent was hot and smelly, the floor grassy. There was a desk, a battered bureau, and a cot. It was nearing nine o'clock. "You don't have to worry about an alarm clock in the morning," Bayard said. "Somebody will wake you up. See you later, fella."

I unloaded my possessions from the Plymouth's backseat into the stuffy tent where bugs were making kamikaze runs on the light bulb. An Underwood Noiseless Portable, elite type, which my mother had given me when I was thirteen years old, went on the rickety desk. I drew some pajamas out of an imitation-alligator-skin suitcase because I feared it might get cold in the night. The imitation-alligator-skin suitcase I had bought at Fort Lawton in Seattle when I was being discharged from the Army. The deathly fear of becoming cold in the night came from winter service in Korea. A pair of smudged white bucks, which I had proudly worn as the

13

badge of a college student, was being tucked under the cot in military style when I felt something strange inside one shoe. It was a note on frilly stationery: "My darling, this is to let you know that no matter how long it takes, I'll be waiting for you. I love you. J."

I sat on the edge of the bed, gazed at the typewriter on the desk, and let myself remember once again. . . .

*

The motel owner in Gatlinburg pushed out the registry book, and I signed my first and middle names, hopefully illegibly. I had moved my college ring around so that only a gold strip showed, a make-believe wedding band. She sat in the Plymouth waiting, the whole operation up to me to pull off. "Yes . . . yes," the man behind the counter said, unable to decipher the name. "Well, Mister—uh—if you two want, join a group of us who sit out back for a little while after dinner. That is, if you get lonesome or anything. We just relax out there, a bunch of us. By that stream out back."

His wife, smiling: "I bet I know what you're up to, son. I've never been wrong yet. It's just written all over the faces of some people."

My heart sank. "What's that, ma'am?"

"You just got married. Now, admit it. Aren't I right?"

In the room that was all ours—our first real room together—she put on her blue robe and prepared to take a shower. I plugged in a radio I was carrying along and lay back on the bed. A mountain stream ran outside; the door in front of me was bolted and chain-locked. By God, I had really pulled it off. I lit a cigarette, and watched her march in from the bathroom, her blue eyes flashing under those dark brows.

"That water's cold," she said. "I'm just not going to stay here unless there's hot water."

I flew to try the faucets. "There's got to be hot water. There's just got to be."

"Try it. . . . See. See."

"O.K., O.K., but what the hell can I do about it?"

"You can go get that manager, and have him look at it."

"Couldn't you take a cold shower?"

"No!"

A few minutes later I came back to the room followed by the motel manager. He turned on the hot water, eyed Juanita in her blue robe, and explained happily, "You have to let the water run a little while before it gets hot. You're the last room from the boiler, and that's why it's cold now. There's nothing wrong here."

"Are you sure it'll get hot?" I said.

"Positively," he said. "And remember. If you want to drop in on us tonight in the backyard, come right ahead. We never embarrass newlyweds."

Soon indeed the water ran hot and Juanita had her shower. I watched her brush her teeth, watched her open her suitcase which she had neatly packed, and felt her cool, moist, marvelous skin. So little did I know about girls, how proud I was to be learning with a girl I loved. I tiptoed from the shower toward the bed, throwing my chest out and sucking in my stomach. We touched, and in seconds were turning and connecting in a multitude of love positions. Back in our hometown we had made love at night in the front and backseat of my car. On cold nights at the drive-in we had taken off every stitch and made love so furiously that the windows steamed up, making a built-in curtain. I had driven onto cow pastures, into woods, and once in front of her house her

15

brother-in-law caught us in *flagrante delicto*. When her parents were away from her house for an hour or two, I rushed over to put it into her someplace immediately. On Sunday afternoon picnics we copulated nude under a blanket. (Once some strollers passed by, and we had to carry on a brief conversation with only our heads sticking out.) As we drove down Main Street, she made love to me in a breathtaking, private way, and I gripped the steering wheel with all my might, terrified someone might spot us at it, afraid she might stop. I feared squads of farmers silently descending on us in a pasture, her mother or father arriving home a few minutes early, an old chum recognizing my car at a drive-in and popping up to say hello. We made love in freezing cold, in spaces no larger than a coffin, and at any hour. Having pulled away from church one bright Sunday, we were connected and moaning five minutes later on a deserted country road.

Now that at last we lay in a real bed with the door barricaded, would we choke up? Not at all. Through glistening sunshine and into pitch-black dark we made love; she was twenty, and I was twenty-three. From out back of the motel came voices from the "party" which sounded tired and middle-aged. In a dazed, relaxed state we finally put on clothes and drove to a restaurant. I couldn't eat but half the fried chicken I had ordered, and she insisted I wrap up the leftovers for my journey to Illinois the next day. "No, I don't want to do that," I said, embarrassed to ask the waitress such a thing. But Juanita insisted. (The next day, when I gnawed at a chicken leg while driving alone, I was thankful.)

Back in the motel she modeled before me in a gauze-thin blue nightdress which allowed her nipples and perfect, curly black triangle to show through faintly. She was able to wear the nightdress for about three minutes, and then we were back at it. At one point I noticed that the "party" noises had ceased out back. And, through the moonlight and the faint light of the radio dial, I watched her sleeping gently on her side. She made absolutely no noise. I turned over for a moment's rest, but soon felt her touching me.

"Good God," she said, "you're ready again!"

"This makes number nine, doesn't it?" I said. "Do you think Kinsey would believe it?"

And I remembered that I had had terrible trouble getting an erection with the first woman I ever put it in—a whore in a hotel. And I thought of the many times in Korea I had spent beside garlic-eating, non-English-speaking girls, lying on grass mats and begging my flaccid member to rise. Now there was no stopping it. It was as if *rigor mortis* had set in. Before I'd known her, I'd never thought of myself as sexy. Sex-driven, but not sexy. She had made me think of myself as a lover.

" . . . you know," I said, sometime near dawn, her head on my chest, "no book or movie or poetry or what anybody says tells you really what this is. But if anyone *had* told me before that it could be like this, I wouldn't have believed it. You ever thought of that? Oh, I love you so, Juanita."

"I love you so, too. I've never been in love before. Please don't ever hurt me."

"I won't. I'll die first."

Eating breakfast in the brightly lit motel coffee shop that morning, we ducked out in a hurry when we thought we saw someone from the hometown. In the room we made love once again, checked out on the run, and then began the drive to Knoxville where I would drop her off before going on to the Writer's Colony. A smell of country fields came through the open windows, and a bluish, sparkling day was rising.

17

She sat near the car door, the breeze fluttering her dark hair. "Look," I said, and magnanimously tossed a gross of unused, tinfoil-wrapped Trojans out the window. "I'll never use them on anybody else. Those were ours."

"I can't imagine ever dating anyone else now," she said, that dramatic ring to her voice. She had wanted to be an actress and had occasionally studied to be one.

"Listen, I'll stay up at that Colony for about three months and that should be long enough to learn everything about how to write. Then I'll come back and we'll get married. But don't hold me back from going up there, darling. Let me have this one chance. Nobody in Tennessee knows anything about writing."

"When you come back, I don't care if we have to live on beans," she said. "We'll get by, because I do so love you."

"Oh, Jesus Christ, I love you so much!"

As we approached the spires of the University of Tennessee, which were dwarfed by nearby Shields-Watkins Stadium, she broke into tears. I held her hand tightly, not speaking, but feeling tears in my own eyes, and with my other hand wheeled up to the bus station. How many emotions, how complicated! I thought of an adventurous, unencumbered drive to Illinois with little stops at bars along the way. But then I thought—while she stood on the steps to the bus station and looked my way—about what would happen if I suddenly opened the door and told her to get back in. I could become a newspaper reporter in Tennessee; we could drive to Hollywood and she could try for the movies while I wrote; we could live in a cold-water flat in New York. Yet, looking at it practically, I knew she might get sore if I didn't stick to my decision: "Can't you ever make up your mind!" or "Don't you know how to do anything right!" She would be proud of me, striking out to become a writer.

I did not open the door, and I drove off slowly from the bus station.

*

Now, under smelly canvas on a narrow cot with the whine of a mosquito in my ear, I closed my eyes. I awoke in a dewy, pearl-gray dawn. A freckled young man with a shaved bullet head had thrown back the tent flap, and was saying, "Five thirty. Time to get up. Five thirty." This was Perc, someone I remembered vaguely from the blur of faces the night before. In the *ramada* I self-consciously followed examples and toasted some raisin bread and poured a mug of Instant Maxwell House. Eggs and bacon were never served here; each man fixed his own breakfast. Perc, whose grayish skin looked reptilian in the early light, suddenly cleared his throat in a deep, rasping thrust that brought a large wad of something I dared not think of to his mouth. But his Adam's apple didn't swallow, nor did he spit. His face took on a momentary color, and that was that. It was not human.

"Are you working on a novel?" I said, to be friendly.

"We never talk about our work here," he said. "And we don't talk to each other here at breakfast. Those are Lowney's rules."

"I'm sorry. I didn't know. I just got here yesterday."

He turned and walked into the screened-in section with its couches and easy chairs and picnic tables. Lowney came out of her white frame house to the rear of the *ramada* following a snap of her screen door. She wore the gray sweat shirt, pushed up at the sleeves and without brassiere, and a loose

19

blue skirt that whirled with her chugging stride. Noticing her frown, I didn't dare speak to her. Last night she had been so sweet and gentle.

"Perc! I want you to drive and get the groceries at Kroger's. We haven't got a fucking thing to eat here!"

(The only female I had ever heard use the word fuck was Juanita in private. It made me a little giddy now to hear an older woman say it.)

"We need cigarettes, Lowney," Perc said in a strangled voice. "We're down to one carton."

"That does it! That son-of-a-bitching smoking is sending us to the poor house. Ten cartons in three days. From now on you bastards roll your own."

"Do you want me to pick up Bugler or Bull Durham?"

"Anything, Perc! Jesus Christ, do I have to wipe your ass for you!"

Whewww! My hand shook, lifting my coffee mug, and I tried to squeeze up and become invisible. Lowney threw open cabinet doors, marched flat-footed around the smooth concrete-floored room, and barked commands: "Two cans of pimentos, five pounds of Irish potatoes, two dozen roastin' ears. . . . Where's that fucking George?"

"I told him to stay in his room today," Bayard said. "His shiner's worse."

"Take something over for him to eat, Bayard." Her glance, swinging around the kitchen, settled on me. Then all at once the storm clouds parted and the sun shone through. Her smile showed perfect, even white teeth. "There's my boy from Tennessee. I'm sure we're related somehow, but I don't know how. Are you getting settled down, honey?"

"Do you want me to write anything this morning?" I blurted out.

"Copy," she said. "Copying'll make you a writer faster than anything. Oh, the things I've learned since Jim Jones walked into my life. He was wearing dark glasses and a trench coat the first time he came over to my house in Robinson. He wanted to read his poetry. La-de-da. I'd heard about him before; I knew he was out on a psycho discharge from the Army. They told me in Robinson that if I let Jim Jones move into my house, I'd end up with my throat slit. I moved him in. He had his own room to work in. And *Eternity* is nothing! It was just an exercise, an adolescent's book. His next one will be the great one. It'll knock those yokels in New York on their ass. They won't understand it. They'll ask where Prewitt is. People will learn to know what it is about without understanding why. That's what it is about all great revolutions. The people learn something and don't know why. But they know. Christ said that if ye have faith of a mustard seed, ye can enter the Kingdom of Heaven. That's all it takes. The faith of a mustard seed. And you can be a great writer. I don't want any slick, half-ass writers. I only want great ones. All you have to have is the faith of a mustard seed."

"Is there anything particular you want me to copy?"

"Copy Hemingway, *The Sun Also Rises*. It's got some of the best dialogue ever written. And copy midway in *Tender is the Night*. Boy, Fitzgerald got inside people, women, the way no other writer has. Leave Tom Wolfe alone. Try some early Caldwell, and parts of *Light in August* by Faulkner. John Dos Passos is one of the greatest living writers we've got. Copy 'Art and Isadora' from *U. S. A.* He can write rings around Hemingway."

"Do you want me to copy all of that?"

"No, copy what you can. But copy, copy, copy. Don't

21

think while you do it. Let it seep in to your brain and it'll stay there. Mary Ann was writing a hell of a fine novel, and it came about through her copying. I don't know whether to go ahead and finish her book or not, I've got so much work to do. . . . Perc! Some cottage cheese, large curds. And I don't want you bringing back small curds like last week."

"Lowney, I told Mr. Bradley three times last week to make sure——"

"Look on the fucking outside of the container, Perc! That's all you have to do. Jesus K. Rist! That's what's wrong with your writing. You fiddle fart around. Thirty fucking pages and you're just posturing and saying, 'Look at me, look at me.' Forget Perc Tasker! Forget he was ever born. Kill that ego. And then rise from your dead ashes like the Phoenix bird. You'll never be a writer until you do. Never, never, never. You'll just be pretending."

Perc knocked a long cigarette ash in his coffee without noticing, and his neck went out like a tortoise, his mouth hanging open.

I went over to my tent and began copying like a madman.

An iron bell clanged vigorously outside the *ramada* at noon, and figures popped out of the screen doors. (The newest arrival, I was the only one in a tent.) Inside the *ramada* we grabbed plastic plates and passed by the stove in a line, helping ourselves to what was in the pots. This day we had boiled potatoes in their jackets, corn on the cob, and a dish with plenty of pimentos in it. Lowney had cooked it all in a whirlwind, but did not stay to eat with us. On the picnic tables were white cardboard buckets of cottage cheese, large-curd style. There was no butter or milk—items I had always been used to at meals. ("Lowney don't like butter on potatoes, or milk to drink. Don't drink any water with your

22

meal, either.") But here I was at last with people who spoke my own language. They didn't care about getting the latest car model, didn't indulge in backslapping, boring talk about nothing, and didn't award any kudos because of someone's money, family background, or the college of your choice. Only one thing apparently mattered: writing as an art and way of life. Sid, an unsmiling blond youth, had a brownish discharge running from his ears. Jud, a balding, thirtyish man in horn-rims, cleared his throat, turned a reddish color, paused with his mouth open slightly, before he spoke his occasional few words. Perhaps only Bayard, with his easygoing manners and cockeyed smile, would have been rushed by any of the fraternities I had been so taken up with only a short time before. But all had a certain humor, all wanted to write another *From Here to Eternity*. There were no girls.

Jim came back from Peoria, and was either in Lowney's bungalow or in his silverish trailer. His Chrysler convertible was now parked under a lean-to near Lowney's black Buick. On the clear, bright day of Mary Ann's funeral, Lowney took me aside. She had on the type of dress worn in the outside world, with a half veil, and it seemed strange on her. "I'm going to leave you behind, honey," she said in her sweet-type voice. "Someone should stay here with George and make sure he doesn't run off to Terre Haute for a spree. I'm leaving you in charge. If you'd known Mary Ann, I'd have made sure you got to go to the funeral."

After the others left, George and I sat around in the *ram-ada*. What should I do if he suddenly suggested a joy flight outside Colony grounds? But he was very contented where he was, talking about his experiences so far in the world of letters. His hometown was near Louis Bromfield's, and once he had gone to that great writer's home, only to be ordered

23

off the grounds. The book he admired most after *From Here to Eternity* (more, if you judged by the manner of his enthusiasm) was *Knock on Any Door* by Willard Motley. "That book's how I see life," he said, rocking back on a picnic table, smoking a pipe. (Jones smoked a pipe now and then, and others had then taken it up.) "A choirboy goes out in the world, and everything fucks him up. Boy, that Motley can really write. If I could write a book like that, I'd be the happiest guy in the world. But don't tell Lowney I said that, will you?"

"O.K., but why not?"

"She thinks Motley is shit. And we're not supposed to talk at all about our books anyhow, you know."

"When do you know you're writing a book? All I've been doing is copying."

"Oh, you'll start doing scenes pretty soon, and before long it'll turn into a book. I'm thinking about a title for my book now. Don't tell anyone, but what do you think of this as a title?" On a white sheet of paper was typed in capital letters and underlined, *FLY FLAGRANT ANGEL.*

I didn't want to suggest its similarity to *Look Homeward, Angel* because I didn't want to hurt his feelings. I had to say something, though. "It's . . . pretty good, I guess. Do you read much Wolfe?"

"Lowney says he's the best at titles. John Dos Passos is the worst. *U. S. A.* would have been the best-known book in America today if it'd had a better title. Who's going to read something that sounds like an atlas? That's what Lowney says."

*

24

A short time after the funeral I was moved from the tent into one of the tiny, tourist-court-type rooms. When my Underwood portable wasn't smoking in use, an old torn T-shirt covered it. Along with everyone else, excepting Lowney, I wrote or tried to, or copied from about seven until the noon chow bell rang. I rewrote a story I had done in college as my first scene. The setting—a Victorian household in Knoxville where a formidable matron had once rented me a room during my junior year—was authentic, but I made up everything that happened. Nothing like it had ever happened in my life, the theme and mood coming straight from Faulkner. Lowney said it was fine, but keep trying.

The next scene took off from a real person I had seen often in my hometown, a grizzled, slightly crazy man, who carried a sandwich board over his body, turtle fashion, which advertised hometown baseball games. He had a walleye, and would spout off about sex in as freewheeling a manner as I'd ever heard an adult do before. Lowney said this was better; much, much better.

Inspired, I did a thirty-page, Erskine Caldwell-type vignette about a salty old man who goes around a small Southern town, lusting after nubile girls and living by his wits.

"Johnny," she screamed in a voice that chilled my blood, flying out of her bungalow and clutching those thirty yellow sheets. "This is just plain awful, awful. People live with more dignity than this. Look at my father. He never went past the seventh grade, but he's got as much dignity as the President of the United States. You could learn a hell of a lot from my Kentucky father. Write the *truth*, Johnny. Cut this other shit out!"

That made me so miserable so quickly that my lips went dry and stayed that way for days. But like the Phoenix bird, I

25

rose from those dead ashes. I sat down one morning not knowing what I would write, and began telling how I had once gone to watch my older brother play in a college-football game. A hard, cold rain had fallen that Saturday afternoon long ago, and I had become soaked to the bone. But I sat there in rapture, watching my big brother run in the mud, throw flying blocks, and tackle around the ankles. Nearby I had heard pretty, desirable college girls talk about him. And there I had sat, a skinny little kid getting soaked and frozen to numbness, and I had walked the three miles home from the stadium in the rain to have my mother draw me a hot bath. During that period in the late Depression, my father had to work out of town to support us. I remember how quietly he came and went from the house—more, it seemed then, as a dignified stranger one must be respectful to than as a conquering hero. But my brother! I had never forgotten my big brother's day of glory that afternoon or how proud I had been to be related to him. But until that moment I began writing about it I never knew how important it was.

"This is just beautiful," Lowney wrote across the top of the manuscript. "Keep it up!"

From that one scene I began a novel about a glorified football player and a younger brother who idolized him and played the guitar. The older brother I named Frank; the younger brother I called Charley Henderson, a name close to that of one of my best friends in college, Charley Hickerson. (Right before my graduation in 1951 Charley and I had gone on a toot without sleep for four days simply to prove we could do it; we kept a steady buzz on from pints of bourbon and gin we carried in hip pockets, but never passed the thin line into blind drunkenness. We had invaded the girls' freshman dorm, and hung a Budweiser portrait of Custer's Last

Stand in the lounge. Wearing tin derbies on a misty early morning, we had mounted horses from a stable off Kingston Pike, and had gone charging beneath tree branches and down pasture hills at a full gallop. Never allowing the derbies to leave our heads, we had eaten steaks in a dim, college hangout, passing the bottle to all the Negro help. From the back of the ATO House we had slung empty beer cans at the passing, bobbing heads of fraternity brothers. Charley was to graduate later at the University, was to go on to Cumberland University Law School, was to become a lawyer and family man in Tullahoma, Tennessee.) So Charley Henderson sprang forth, a moony boy who delivered groceries on a bicycle, idolized and feared his big brother, and picked up guitar playing to impress a neighbor girl. His father was a businessman, gruff, bald-headed, and nosey—everything my own father was not. Charley thirsted after fame or to live in its reflected glow. I didn't consciously will him into being; he just appeared.

"O.K., everybody," Lowney said one day in the *ramada* kitchen, "look over there at that boy. That boy from Tennessee. He's learned faster how to write than any pupil I've ever had before. He's writing a book now. It's going to be a great book."

The Phoenix bird never flew so high. Now I started becoming temperamental. The walls separating our tiny cells were thin as cardboard, and sounds from up and down the line filtered through. There were sporadic bursts from typewriters, like machine-gun reports in jungle warfare. Occasionally came coughs and the screech of chairs moving back and forth, and books being dropped or thrown. Now and then a belch or cough or wind being broken sounded. In the room beside me George labored. No sooner had the announcement gone out that I was the fastest learner in the place than he began barking out dialogue from his work in progress before banging it out on the typewriter. "Listen, you little punk shit," came a hoarse voice, "I'm throwing you in the pokey, and you can see how *that* sits with your ass."

"Oh, Phil"—in a girlish falsetto—"don't take off my panties! Oh, don't get on me like that! Ooooh, what a big one!"

And from out of the side of his mouth came, "O.K., Sam, drop the gat. This ain't my finger I'm sticking in your back."

I would wait and wait (in vain) for the answering line of dialogue, my hands poised above my typewriter keys, my brain fogging up. Finally, I would sock my fist against the typewriter and pace the cell; then I would barge out to sip water at the spigot and take a leak in the outdoor privy. At least four or five times a morning I would be swept away with a longing to stretch out flat on my back and snooze. But I feared Perc or Bayard passing by and reporting me. (My comment about "prostituting myself in a middle-class job" had been passed on to Lowney and also the fact that I had a loving girl friend back in Tennessee.) Sex fantasies concerning Juanita danced in and out of my brain like malaria attacks, and I daydreamed about being rich and famous and desired in Hollywood. We were at our typewriters in the morning seven days a week and we never observed a holiday. The Fourth of July was like any other day.

"Listen," I said to George one day, in my role as the Fastest Learner in the Colony, "couldn't you be a little quieter in the mornings when you work? I can hear you talking to yourself."

The smile shy, enigmatic as so much of him was. "I sometimes get carried away," he said. The sounds from his cubicle did not lessen, and I had to adjust as best I could.

Always at noon, without fail, came the respite. Jones' trailer door would creak open, close with a snap, and he would plow toward the *ramada*, a martini tumbler with lemon twist in his hand like a grail. Dressed in shorts or Levi's with sandals, his chest most often bare, he moved through the chow line like everyone else. Before I spoke to him, I went over in my mind every sentence I would use. And when he answered, I was so goofily tense that I had trouble straightening out his words into a clear meaning. Here, this man with sandy hair, who came to my shoulders, was the man who had written *Eternity*. He knew the secret; he was better than I was.

"That's an unusual wristband you've got there, Jim," I croaked once, sitting opposite him at the chow table. "What's that stone in it?"

"It's turquoise. I got it out West." He then went into its history, touching on an Indian tribe in Arizona and the stone's meaning in a tribal ritual. His voice was gentle, patiently explaining esoteric facts. When he ate, his whole hand gripped his fork, palm down, and he leaned over to within inches of his food. Frequently he removed his bridgework and sucked out hidden slivers of meat there. Burps rolled at the table, fingers were licked of grease, and once in a great while came the report of a fart fired backwards toward the screen. We were taught to have no hang-ups about the bathroom. "The fucking mothers of this country have made us all ashamed of our body's functions," Jones would say. "Everybody is terrified of being human."

"You should take an enema," Lowney would say to anyone complaining of feeling bad. "I've seen it work wonders. Wonders. If you'd get all that shit out of your system, then maybe you could write a fucking novel."

We seldom talked about sex at the table, and never when Lowney was there. It was as if it didn't exist—as it's supposed not to exist in insane asylums and prisons. And only rarely did we mention our writing, always with bitter results.

"Jim," George said once, out of nowhere, "why did you let Prewitt get killed? Couldn't you have let something else happen to him? It don't seem right."

"Sure," Jones said, wheeling, eyes flashing. "I could have elected him President of the United States. Would that have satisfied you?"

"Well, it just seemed a shame——"

"Worry about your own fucking book!"

And tripping in about once a week for a meal came Lowney's wisp of a mother-in-law, Mrs. Handy, who was nearing ninety and who was writing a novel herself. She lived alone in a two-story Victorian home which was down a hill and across a small stream from the Colony. It seemed a strong gust of wind would blow her away, and she kept a faint smile on her thin lips because of bad hearing, but she was the only one ever to penetrate the Colony whom Lowney seemed to hold in some fear. "That's a tough old biddy," Lowney would say, rushing between pots and pans in the kitchen. "She fought tooth and nail to keep me from marrying Harry. Of course you'd never suspect it now, the way it's all sweetness and light with her. But I'm not trusting her one little inch. She may come out, though, with a hell of a book. God knows she's got one in her."

Lowney always gave Mrs. Handy one of her dazzling white smiles, but she never passed much more than the social amenities with her.

In the hot, drowsy afternoons we did physical labor around the Colony. For a long stretch we "cleaned" old bricks of mortar and then used the bricks to line the gigantic crater that someday would be a mammoth swimming hole. Harry Handy ran an oil refinery well away from the cloister of the Colony. Bulldozers from the refinery had shoveled out the dirt; refinery dump trucks had delivered the used bricks. Silver-haired Harry, in natty sports attire, overlooked the delivery of bricks or some other chore done by men from his refinery. He would stand straight, hands on hips, a black cigarette holder sticking out of the side of his mouth. Periodically he would wheel around, slip to the glove compartment of his Buick, and take a long drink from a pint he always had there. By twilight he weaved with hands on hips, his words slurred.

At the "rock pile" we phlegmatically whacked away with hammers at the old crusty mortar, tossed bricks at each other, and shot the breeze. We talked of writers who were acceptable at the Colony (Hemingway, Faulkner, Dos Passos; never T. S. Eliot, Proust, or Camus.) Old-timers passed yarns about eccentric Colony members who had left the fold; newcomers asked sly questions about what to expect in the weeks to come. One bit of intelligence that immediately flamed the mind was the news that about once a month Lowney let the troops go into Terre Haute for an evening. There were bars there, whorehouses (*"Real* whorehouses, man. A whole block-long of 'em!"), and movies. In the Colony there were no TV sets, no radios, no newspapers, no magazines. "They're all filled with lies," Lowney said. The Korean War had been on for a couple of weeks before the Colony knew about it.

With brick dust going up my nostrils I saw exactly how a bottle of beer would look in its natural habitat: beads of sweat running down a brown bottle; a cool, damp-smelling bar; a jukebox churning away. Under my sheet at night I saw

31

a whore out there waiting for me with a girl-next-door look. During the night hours and often shortly before the five-thirty reveille, there would be telltale snappings of Lowney's and Jim's screen doors. You did not ask questions about what those door snappings meant. So much was explained at the Colony—the efficacy of copying, enemas, hot Jell-o, the subtlety of Hemingway dialogue, the truthfulness of Fitzgerald's insights, the superiority of Far Eastern philosophers ("Masters of the Far East") over those of the West—that the mind reeled and much went unspoken. Inhibitions were switched around in me and many others, and what was Good and Bad in the outside world was not necessarily so inside the Colony. We said fuck, shit and piss and were allowed graciously to delineate how our mothers had wrecked our lives—but we feared growing our hair long ("I don't want any son of a bitch here thinking he's Tom Wolfe!"), getting our heads crew cut about twice a month, and it was drilled into those of us who were vulnerable that marriage was the kiss of death to an Artist.

Lowney on women: "I don't care who they are, they're out to fill that womb with a child. They look around to this man and that, looking for one who can make the best nest for them in order to have that child. It's in the woman's *nature*, you poor bastards, and you don't see it ever. You think a woman spends her time listening to Chopin and reading Shelley and being wooed with roses. You think she's *romantic?* Bullshit. A woman is the most cold-blooded creature on earth when it comes to selecting a man. She spends every hour of the day in the process. She wants to know how much money that man is going to bring in in his lifetime, how strong he will be in protecting that nest, how a baby by him will fare. You poor sons-a-bitches. You think women are delicate and need protection, but that's a myth created by a matriarchal society. Women have you by the balls, all of you, and you never have figured it out. I'll tell you something else, too. There's no difference in desires between a man and woman in bed. A woman is just as hot in the sack as a man and always gets as much pleasure . . . but for centuries she's had you believing that she's getting the dirty end of the stick and you must pay for fucking her. Pay and pay and pay. . . . A man who gets married and becomes a Householder will never be an Artist. An Artist must carry the Yellow Begging Bowl, as the Masters of the Far East say, and go from house to house. . . . "

That turned a lifetime of noble feelings around at least a half circle. How *good* I had felt in the past when I told Juanita I loved her more than life itself, and that I would protect her for always; now how *bad* I felt that I had possibly been tricked. In those romantic, halcyon pre-Colony days I had sometimes thought she might be playing a part (her actress training, you know), but still it had *felt* good when I said I would sacrifice anything for her happiness. But didn't Lowney have to be right about all this? Didn't she get *From Here to Eternity* written?

Juanita wrote:

Darling, are you warm enough? Is Lowney feeding you enough food? Please forgive me for asking these things, but I worry about you. And do answer these questions I ask. I do want to know. It's dull here now without you. I see movies with girl friends, play with the dog, eat meals with my parents. . . . Oh, I miss you so much. My mind misses you, my heart misses you, my body misses you. Oh, I can't wait until fall comes and you've finished your book. Will we forever make that dern bed squeak! 'A couple of honeymooners,' the people in the room next door

33

will say. My brother knows I'm getting close to twenty-one and keeps calling me an Old Maid. I feel like one too. But I'm proud of you, darling, I really am. I don't care either if you have to do it up there with a whore for money—just as long as you don't catch a disease. But don't fool around with any country girls up there, the kind who make you wait three months before you can put a finger in them.

Why had I had the bad luck to have had this affair right before coming to the Colony? If I had been completely ignorant of her and what a love affair was like, then I could concentrate wholeheartedly on learning how to write. Now I sweated in guilt. At night, lying on my bunk and listening to high-volume cricket sounds, I visualized driving up to her place in Tennessee on the spur of the moment. Perhaps she would be sneaking in a date with some guy. I wouldn't put it past her. But I confidently saw no trouble in immediately taking her away from the other man. No one else ever could share with her those moments we'd had in the backseat of a car, on the ground under a blanket, and on a bed in a motel room. She had told me about a guy before my time, someone from a neighboring town who used to take her to his own home, wait until his parents were snoring fast asleep upstairs, then slip off her panties from beneath her dress and quietly go about his business like a surgeon. What exquisite torture that story had been! I would never be able to see what the guy looked like—he would never meet me in a fight—because he went off to join the Navy and married someone else. But since he had come before my time, I was forced to build him up in my imagination. So now I would take this person's place to anyone who might come along in Juanita's life. That faceless agent would never know exactly what Juanita and I had done together. Once, on my birthday, she had come out on a date with me with no panties on. What breathtaking delight to reach down and discover that fact at the old drive-in with no warning. It was a love gift. "Just another little present for you, darling," she had said. After such as that, how could anyone take her away from me?

*

We were sitting at the chow table in the *ramada*. A fly buzzed over the steaming ears of corn, a shaft of sunlight came through the screen, and our talk was relaxed and funny. Jones had taken off for one of his dental appointments; Lowney had cooked our meal and immediately gone back to her bungalow. Then suddenly came that smart snap of her screen door, the sound of her moccasined feet going *crunch crunch* on the gravel, the kitchen screen door flung open and shut, and her feet slapping the cement floor and coming straight for us. We all shut up guiltily.

"All right, which one of you guys was reading this book?" And she slammed a volume of the Masters of the Far East down on the table beside the bowl of large-curd cottage cheese. A dark angry flush was covering her face, and the whites of her eyes stood out like Al Jolson's in blackface.

No one spoke at the table. Forks stopped, and eyes sought out safe objects to gaze at intently. Slowly one face began changing from its natural grayish shade to a purplish red. George ducked his head, hunched his shoulders as if trying to squeeze up into the smallest possible ball. His feet moved under the table, possibly warming up for flight.

"All right. Whoever had this book knows what I'm talking about," Lowney said. "And I want him to know that I tore up

35

that picture into a million pieces. I'd better never catch any of you with any of those pictures—*ever again*! I'm not going to have any queers in this Colony!"

George's upper bridge shot out of his mouth and was drawn back in by his tongue.

"*What am I going to do?* I give up my life, my own book, the respect of all my friends in Robinson, just to try to teach you bastards something from forty-some-odd years of my experience. AND this is the thanks I get! Get out of here. Go to Terre Haute. I don't want to see one of your faces around here today. I want a complete vacation from every one of you!"

"Lowney, does this mean there won't be any shopping this afternoon at Kroger's?" Perc asked.

"Of course, Perc! Go. *Go. GO!*"

In a matter of minutes we showered, shaved, put on regular street clothes that felt and looked strange on our bodies. Possibly she would change her mind at the last moment, halt my car from leaving the gate, inform us that we really didn't deserve a day off and must go back to the brick pile. But miraculously the car sped down the gravel road, took off up a shady tree-lined street of Marshall, and then pointed itself like an arrow for Terre Haute. I flicked on the radio for music from the outside. A sweet summerish breeze whipped in through open windows. The car was jam-packed, and George sat huddled by the window. He wore a sport shirt of the bargain-basement green color, and drops of water still hung to his hair from the recent combing. "Man, I sure fouled up this time," he said.

"What the hell was in that picture?"

"Aw—nothing. A girl sucking this guy off, I think. Shit, I used it as a bookmark and forgot about it."

"You're stupid," Bayard drawled from the backseat. "You're the only one so dumb as to leave a fuck picture as a bookmark in the Masters of the Far East. She should kick you out."

"I'm sorry, guys."

We were all silent, some of us thinking about pornographic pictures of our own and thankful that there hadn't been a wallet inspection at the chow table. In Terre Haute we were led by the veteran Colony members into a pleasantly air-conditioned bar that had a nautical motif. Soon martinis and beers and mixed drinks covered our table, and we were happily regaling each other with drinking and literary yarns, sometimes both combined. "You know, they say Faulkner goes on toots where they have to feed him through his veins. . . . " "Hemingway never writes a line when he's drinking. . . . " "I get the urge sometime to go off to Greenwich Village, grow a beard and write by candlelight. Wonder what the Masters of the Far East would say about that?"

There was nothing quite like that first martini. Taking the first tiny sip and feeling it spread out hotly below, the whole day and coming evening lay waiting out there to be enjoyed as it never had before. Freedom. No copying, writing, rock pile, large-curd cottage cheese, and Jell-o. Everyone at our table shared the secret and had the same humor. We were Outsiders to the world, we knew the Truth, and we felt a Brotherhood. The second and third martinis didn't taste quite as well and began making one light-headed. We lurched out of the nautical bar, strangers glancing at us oddly. A few in our group went to movies, George suddenly disappeared, and others of us stumbled into a subterranean, working-class bar. Over beer, our minds turned lightly to thoughts of pussy. "There was this girl I used to know in high school," Bayard drawled, "who was the sweetest little thing you ever saw. Well, she got married and I didn't see her for a while. Then one day I run into her in a supermarket, and she invites me up to her house. Two hours later we were fucking on her bed. God damn, what a woman! I was running over there every minute she was free. Who'd have thought that of her in high school? Whoowee, could she fuck."

Nelms, a hairy-chested man and veteran of the Occupation in Germany, told about the maturity and availableness of European women.

The beer made the head swim, and the bottles became harder to down. On a trip to the toilet I spied a wall phone. I called collect. ("Darling, I know you don't have much money up there—so just call collect. I can't wait to hear your voice.") She was out, but was expected in soon. Then, after another beer, here was her high, unmistakable voice. "Oh, darling, are you eating well? Are you getting a day off? Tell me, tell me."

"I love you. . . . We're all getting drunk here in Terre Haute. . . . I miss you, baby. . . . I'm writing O.K."

"What are you writing about now? Tell me."

"Something new. . . . Oh, the guys are leaving this place, sweetheart. Look, I'll call you at the next spot."

"How long? I'll wait here."

"Fifteen or twenty minutes. I love you."

"I love you."

A Colony veteran led us to Cherry Street. At the back door of a structure a dim light shone underneath a buzzer. The door was flat and as sturdy-looking as a bank's. The buzzer could be heard rasping inside, and almost immediately a short, skinny woman, ugly enough to still any passion,

38

opened up with a clank of metal. "We've been here before," one of the vets announced. "Remember me?"

"I remember you. You haven't been drinking too much, have you?"

"Nope."

"How old is this one?"

"Twenty-one. You want to see his ID?"

"I take your word."

We were permitted to urinate first in a large toilet area that could have been transferred to any barroom, and we hooted and tingled in nervousness. In an area that resembled a doctor's waiting room, complete with magazines and non-descript prints on the walls, we sat subdued. Then, like a scene in some play, the girls entered from behind closed doors: a well-built brunette in a peekaboo harem ensemble; a hard-faced woman in a slit skirt and heels; a languid redhead in a bathrobe; and then a pale, pretty blonde with blue bows in her hair. They took positions, and we all talked politely for a while as if we had just dropped by for a chat. "Where you boys from?" the hard-faced woman asked. "Off a farm?"

"No, we're writers," one of us said proudly. "We're with Jim Jones over in Marshall. You ever hear of the Colony over there?"

"Oh, yeah, I heard something about it. I liked that book he did—what was it?—The Naked and the Something or Other. It was O.K. . . . All right," she said abruptly, hand to hair, "who wants a date?"

In Tennessee you are taught to move immediately when either whisky or women offer themselves, because a second chance doesn't present itself often. I moved past the hard-faced woman and took the blonde. Mainly because she hadn't spoken.

39

In a room with shiny linoleum on the floor and a well-worn pink spread on the bed she unzipped her frock and got down to panties and bra. I stripped too, with few words. After an exchange of five dollars, she filled a tin washbowl with sudsy water and began soaping my genitals in a bored, detached way as if she were a nurse. It was exciting in that impersonal manner, and continued to be so as she dried me off with a rough towel. "O.K., baby," she said, striking a pose on the sad bedspread, "how do you want it?"

How did I want it? Had I missed out on some secret? (Later I was to learn that the way to get the most fancy treatment in the house was to ask for a "half and half.") "The usual," I said. There was a pained expression from her when I demanded that I use an ancient condom from my billfold.

"You don't have to use a rubber in this house," she said. "I'm clean."

"I'd just feel better if I used one."

While I mounted her, I politely asked where she came from. She came from Memphis. Fancy that. We were from the same state. We chatted pleasantly while business went on down below as usual. It was as if it would be bad manners to connect her mind with her pussy—and I pretended not to notice the phallus that plunged in and out of her. But in a quiet, sociological manner it was all right to ask how she got into the trade. "Oh, I just sort of fell into it," she said, then added angrily in a new voice, "are you going to come or are you going to take all night?"

"Just a little while longer."

"Listen, we can't stay in this room for hours, others are waiting their turns." A couple of licks, and then out of the blue: "O.K., big boy, give it to me, give it to me!"

I knew she was lying, but still it had excited me. Now I

wished that I had chosen the hard-faced woman or the girl in the harem costume. But my buddies would tell me what they had been like and I would get double my money's worth. Right now they were battering around in adjoining rooms. Just as I made my last thrust, the blonde from Memphis whirled off the bed, did a dipping motion, and washed herself in the tin washbowl that had recently served my own genitals. Possibly in the same water. Back in her clothes in a flash, she hurried me into mine, and then saw that I got out the door. The others were lounging around in the sitting room, sheepish grins on their faces.

We all left the house with a tired, satisfied swagger. In the back room of a bar we dug into shrimp, washed down by beer that now had lost its zing, listening to Hank Williams music on the jukebox. My eyelids had trouble staying up, and the tabletop beckoned my forehead the way a library school desk used to in the old days when I grew uncontrollably sleepy. And then one of the veterans was shaking me upright. "You gotta stay awake, man. You're the fucking driver!"

It came to me in slow-motion waves; there was something I should do. Outside of being respectful to family and trying to make good grades in school solely for them, what other responsibilities had I ever shouldered? Not many. Once I had been scared of Army officers and had served as a soldier. Now I feared Lowney Handy and Jim Jones. But there was something driving me to the phone. Wouldn't it be just as well to write her that I couldn't get a connection and had to drive back to the Colony? Wouldn't she always be waiting by the phone? Wasn't it better to leave the endearments the way we had spoken them a few hours earlier? It had been so romantic, perfect. No, I remembered suddenly . . . I had told her I would call her back, and I had better do so.

"Hello," I said, Hank Williams blaring beside me. "Hello, darling, I'm back again."

"Where have you been? I've been waiting here all evening."

"It's been hard to get to a phone. . . . I told you I'm out with the guys from the Colony; it's not so easy to get to a phone. . . . " My head was swimming; it was difficult to comprehend what she was saying. "Listen, tell me, bay-BEE. . . . Let me hear it."

" . . . I love you."

"And will you wait for me?"

"Always."

All the riders in the backseat fell asleep on the drive back. While a large, clear moon shone ahead, I steered toward home with a can of beer in one hand and a Pall Mall between the fingers of the other. The Colony, washed in moonlight, was still and deathlike as I rolled in on the gravel. Jim's Chrysler was parked snugly by Lowney's black Buick. Lights were off. I woke my fellow celebrants up, and we went alone to our individual cells.

*

There came unexpected moments when Jones absented himself from the Colony. One evening he would be wearing Levi's and engineer's boots, talking about Faulkner. In the morning he would be wearing his two-toned shoes, suit with pants jacked up by suspenders, and a straw hat resting flatly on his head. He would be off to Chicago, St. Louis, or out West on a hunting spree—but no hint ever that he was taking off after women. It would have been unthinkable to articulate such a thought in front of Lowney. "Be careful, Jamie," Lowney would call in her "sweet" voice, as Jones pulled away on the gravel in his Chrysler.

Once he returned from a hunting trip out West with a bagged deer. The meat was cut by a local butcher, stored in a local warehouse freezer, and we were served venison steaks as often as we could stomach them. They weren't so good. The thought that was supposed never to leave our minds was that Jones was a Success. He could travel anywhere he wanted (as long as he came back soon); he could buy anything on the spur of the moment (as long as it could be brought back to the Colony); and what he said was true and important (as long as Lowney didn't correct him). He went into a local bar one day and became fascinated with its shuffleboard game. Soon a shuffleboard game was delivered to the Colony, its zinging bells and flashing colored lights becoming a standard part of the *ramada*. He saw the movie, *The Greatest Show on Earth*, in which circus performers were shown leaping joyfully on a trampolin. In short order a white canvas trampolin arrived by express one day and was set up in a grassy area by the *ramada*. Not long afterwards some of us, Jones included, were able to do flips and half gainers in the air while others stood stationed around the contraption to keep the performer from flipping off and breaking his neck. It could get a little scary on that trampolin.

There were boxing gloves. One afternoon—chest bare, head swathed in a leather protection device—Jones fought George beneath some shade trees. George came in swinging wildly, face red, a grin that never left him plastered on. Jones kept his right cocked, easily warding off George's roundhouse throws; then, suddenly, he would batter George in a crisp one-two. Afterwards, he would explain what he had done and tell George how he should fight. "Keep that right up, like this. No one can hit you if you do. Jab with that left!" But George kept swinging crazily, his goofy smile never leaving him as Jones knocked blood and snot up into the trees. Jones was the Champ.

There were pearl-handled cowboy pistols—souvenirs of a Western jaunt—and Jones spent hours practicing a gunfighter's draw. He could outdraw anybody in the Colony. There was a photo darkroom installed beside the *ramada*, soon forgotten and left to the mice. And then there were the motorcycles.

Bayard came roaring in one day on a black Harley-Davidson, accompanied by a local housebuilder (with no pretensions towards writing and therefore treated kindly by Lowney) on a shiny red Indian. They circled around the white gravel beside the *ramada*, the beasts they straddled emitting earsplitting blasts. Jones was out of his trailer like a shot, rubbing his jaw, eyes transfixed. You knew immediately who would have a motorcycle before another day passed. . . .

The motorcycle he bought was a tan Harley with gleaming silverish crome. To complete the picture, Jones bought a black leather jacket with silver studs and a cyclist's cap. Nearly every afternoon he would roar off with Bayard and the local man for speed runs on highways and tricky maneuvering on little-used country roads. Then he would regale us with motorcycle tales at the dinner table.

Somewhere along the line an old, battered Harley was picked up for the rest of us. Perhaps Lowney dictated that others should be given their chance at riding too; Jones never allowed anyone else to board his beautiful tan Harley. The scarred blue Harley that was purchased came backfiring into the Colony one bright afternoon, Bayard on its wide leather seat with a beatific glow on his face. "She only cost fifteen dollars," he said.

"Now, listen, you guys," Lowney said. "I want you to listen carefully to what Bayard and Jim tell you about driving this thing. No fucking racing, you hear? The first one of you gets hurt, I'm going to destroy all of these machines. And that goes for Jim's bike too. You understand that!"

Jim took charge of showing us how to give gas, how to put on the brake, and how to guide it by leaning the body—with Bayard close by to clarify and emphasize points. "Just remember that this here thing is the brake," Jim said. "You ain't going to get hurt as long as you remember that."

"And jump off if she starts to slide," Bayard chimed in. "Don't get caught under her."

"I rue the fucking day you discovered motorcycles, Jim Jones," Lowney said. "I ought to kick your ass, Bayard, for bringing one in here."

"Aw, Lowney, nobody's going to get hurt. These guys'll learn what to do. We're teaching 'em properly."

"Shit."

Jim took a turn around the gravel, astride the bike like a bull. Bayard made the circle too, standing on the seat in a trick maneuver to demonstrate how easy and safe everything was. No one was conned; everyone of us non-motorcycle drivers had adrenalin and fear streaking through his body like a broken water-main. The most ostensively fearful one was George—his hands and knees trembling, his face flaming—and he was picked by Jones to go first. Calling on some hidden core of courage, he shot a leg over the brute, settled

45

in, and gave it gas. It sprang forth, backfiring, and then slowed into a wobbly, nervous, sputtering run around the course. When he returned to the group, he was full of the giddy hysteria that comes from conquering in front of others a paralyzing terror. "Let me go around again," he said, in a maniacal way. "There's nothing to this."

"I told you so," Jim said. "Now get off and give somebody else a shot."

Two went before I did—which didn't calm my nerves, only making sure I would be horribly shamed if I should fail. I kept telling myself like a prayer, "Turn gas on to the left, shut if off to the right." The gas was attached to the right handlebar, and the brake could be applied by prongs that stuck out from each handlebar. The machine felt hot between my grasping skinny legs, and I threw on the gas. It leaped forward like a horse suddenly kicked, and I drew back on the gas quickly. The motor died. Then I went through the rigamarole of trying to start it with the kick-pedal. I couldn't. Bayard had to do it, and then turn it back over to me. This time I gently eased on the gas, and felt the monster lumber forth. It was soon going faster than I wanted, but I commanded myself not to panic. *Gas to the left, cut off to the right.* I took it twenty-five yards or so, made a broad circle, and roared back to the group. "God, this is fun!"

"Told you so! O.K., Perc, your turn. Climb on and go!"

Perc's face had become a newspaper gray, and even his freckles seemed to have been drained of color. His lips now had the pale hue of someone who has been submerged for hours in water. Without a word or a nod, he slung a leg over. His eyes were glazed, and he had no questions. "You understand, don't ya, Perc? Gas to the left, cut off to the right. The brakes is right here. It's simple," Jim concluded. *"Go!"*

Sitting ramrod straight, his knees out to the sides, Perc turned the gas throttle to the left—and froze. We watched him sail over a beach chair, knock down the canopy to Jim's trailer, miss a water spigot by inches, snap off tree branches with his head. Still perched ramrod straight and heading right for the hill that led down to old Mrs. Handy's place.

"Turn the gas to the right," Jim screamed. "TO THE RIGHT, PERC!"

"Brake it, Perc. BRAKE IT!"

"JUMP, JUMP!"

He shot over the hill, head still high, and disappeared like a pebble down a well. As we ran to the hill, we could hear the motorcycle still roaring away. Perc was rising on one knee, his mouth open and eyes unseeing, while ten feet away from him the blue scarred motorcycle churned impotently on its side.

"Are you hurt, Percie? Are you hurt?" Lowney yelled.

"No."

"Didn't ya hear me telling you to turn the gas to the right?" Jim said, hooting. "That's the funniest sight I ever seen."

"You just *froze*, Perc!" someone else said, hooting along with Jim, and soon most of us were turning our heads in uncontrollable giggles.

"Who's laughing? It's not *funny*," Lowney said. "He could have been killed. I knew something like this was going to happen. I knew it. No more motorcycles. I don't want to hear one more motorcycle sound on these grounds!"

"Aw, Lowney," Jim growled, "these ain't boys. This is the only way to learn 'em. Perc should get right back on and try her again."

"*No!*"

"My knee hurts a little bit, Jim," Perc said. The color that had been coming back to his cheeks drained immediately away.

"I've sunk a fortune into this place," Jim growled, slipping into a favorite theme. *"I get no thanks a-tall."*

"If you didn't have me, you'd never spend a penny!" Lowney said. "Your money would all go to waste. You're the tightest son of a bitch who ever lived!"

"I'm paying for this fucking Colony!"

Jim off to his trailer in blazing anger, laced with guilt; Lowney off in a wiggly, hell-bent stride to her bungalow; the rest of us dragging ourselves to our tiny cells with Perc hawking his throat and nothing coming up, the motorcycle craze stilled for the moment. It didn't occur to any of us that Jim and Lowney might possibly be entangled in some complicated sort of relationship that benefited by having us around or that we really weren't geniuses and that Lowney and Jim and Harry weren't helping us out of the magnificence of their souls. We delved into sex and matrimony and the evils of motherhood—but no one ever really probed into what we were doing at the Colony. Each of us, after a while, got an official-looking, framed document that stated we were members of the Handy Colony. We were told, once in a great while, that Lowney would receive ten percent of anything we published while at the Colony—but that was no more than a regular agent's fee and she didn't seem to care at all about money our books might bring her. She *did* seem to want to get us published—and in a hurry.

"They say I had a lucky fluke with Jim Jones," she often said, "but I'll show 'em. I'll show 'em I can do it with anyone, *anyone* at all." This statement, though, appeared more directed to Jim than to "them." She seemed to want to prove to him that she had the magical touch, that she could bestow this gift on others, and that he (Jim Jones) would be sunk without her. If she *could have* plucked best sellers and great works from that motley crew we had assembled, God knows she would have proved her point.

To know that Jones was entitled to all the trappings of success—to live anyplace he chose and to meet anyone he wanted—made one wonder at times why he put up with the Colony, which afforded large-curd cottage cheese as a staple and the pleasure of batting the breeze with the world's most unfulfilled writers. Possibly he believed he *had* to continue the routine he had kept while writing *Eternity*—Spartan, uncomfortable, angry—else he couldn't pull off another. Or did guilt and a sense of loyalty keep him there? There was the way he rubbed his jaw and lowered his eyes the times Lowney recounted their early days together. Perhaps the reasons were diffuse and complex. He never told us.

No one lasted at the Colony who had a strong personal point of view. Those without fear and those who violated taboos soon got short shrift from Lowney. Once some bearded University of Chicago students came by quoting T. S. Eliot, and were promptly tossed out by Lowney throwing bricks at them. But she could be charming. Burroughs Mitchell, Jim's editor at Scribner's, dropped in for a few days to look at his author's new manuscript. Lowney had sweet, deceptive smiles for him, and kept him away from the contamination of the troops, as if we were poor relations. But we caught glimpses of the Scribner editor—a real live New Yorker from the mysterious publishing world—sipping martinis on Lowney's porch, sipping martinis in Jim's trailer, coming out of the red guest trailer in a neat blue sport shirt that hadn't faded yet from many launderings. Heretofore, I had pictured

New York editors as faceless beings with golden circles over their heads, who didn't have human wants, who feared nothing, who disdained everything. But here was a slim guy in an open-neck shirt, looking lost and swigging booze. A New Yorker.

Through the Fourth of July and into the wavy heat of August, Lowney kept dubbing me Her Fastest Learner. To make myself race to a typewriter I told myself that writing would soon allow me to start laying movie stars, swimming in heated Hollywood pools, and swatting tennis balls on a cinnamon-colored court. Meanwhile the letters from Juanita, as counterpoint, increased in size and anguish. Once Lowney came to me at the lunch table, stuck a bulging pink envelope under my nose, and said, twinkling, "There was six cents due on this one. Boy, she's getting carried away. You better watch yourself."

I wrote Juanita, telling her that she must watch postage in the future because otherwise her letters would be called to Lowney's attention. Then I felt horribly guilty. Alone at night, the moon outside my cell window, I fantasized such items as fornicating with her in a roadhouse parking lot, eating a supper she had prepared, and roaring up a church aisle with her to the Mendelssohn standard. It was an innocent state I dwelt in. Surprises and more surprises were to follow.

We sat happily at lunch—Jones away at the dentist—when Lowney's screen door slapped in the distance. Then the padding of slippered feet, deathly silence at the table, and her presence. She was not smiling. "Everybody comes and asks me why I don't throw George out of the Colony. They say he's a psychopathic liar, that he causes nothing but trouble, and that he's too immature to be taught a fucking thing. God knows he probably never went past the sixth grade and by all rights he should have ended up in the penitentiary. But I want everyone here to know one thing. George is the best writer I've got." She whacked a pile of manuscript down on the table. "He's turning in work now that puts every one of you to shame. He's a hundred percent better than you guys who've been to college and who have been with me for years. Yes, I mean George. Of all the people who have come to this Colony, he is The One Who Most Reminds Me of the Early Jim Jones. That's all I wanted to say."

George blushed, giggled, and ducked his head. Three days later Bayard disappeared from the Colony. Reports came back that he had taken to his sickbed in Robinson. Jim began giving private boxing lessons to George. Now when George rattled off dialogue in his room, blocking me in my own sad creations, I couldn't complain. Who could complain about the one who reminded Lowney the most of the Early James Jones? We never read each other's works; Lowney's judgments were final.

What did it matter if you were Her *Fastest* Learner, when it was so much grander to be Her *Second* James Jones?

I was sitting on the cool cement steps of the *ramada* one sultry August day when a wafer-thin pink envelope was handed me—correct postage affixed.

Dear John:

Although I have not written you this before, I have been dating others now for the last two weeks. I have finally had to come to the conclusion that you want to be alone with your work and prefer to be without me. Perhaps if I were less of a woman I could put up with it, but I can't, darling. I still love you in my own way, but I will not write to you again. I'm now going to try to start a new life without you. Remember, please, the good times . . .

Someone sitting nearby said something, but I could only shake my head. I walked over to Mrs. Handy's and back. I could get in my car, drive all that night, and be in Tennessee early the next evening. Perhaps in time to catch someone taking her out on a date. He was like a New York editor, someone impossible to picture with a face. Or better I could slip into town, without permission, and call her. I would have to do something. The unthinkable had happened, and I had to find relief.

As I walked aimlessly around, shaking my head, a Colony member said, "Let's make some ice cream this afternoon. We haven't had any for some time."

Before I knew it I was furiously turning the handle on the ice-cream mixer. Two times that summer we had made ice cream, and the product had been unbelievably creamy and delicious. I'll just churn this thing till I work off some energy, I thought, and then I'll make a beeline into town. But when the handle became hard to turn, I decided to stick around until the results were known. It would be a shame to check out early.

The thick vanilla ice cream that hot afternoon was the best ever, and I had to spend hours resting up. That evening I postponed slipping into town until tomorrow. By the next day it wasn't too difficult to postpone the call to Juanita a little longer. If I could forget about her for a while and quit penning her long emotional letters, maybe my work would get better. . . .

Weeks passed. . . .

We are again at the lunch table over boiled potatoes and corn, both commodities without butter, when a small package is dropped by my plastic plate in the mail delivery. Eyes turn my way, demanding that I unwrap and show whatever it is. There are few entertainments at the Colony. "Lord, I wonder what she's sent me this time," came from my lips.

It was a watch, and it was from my mother. She had remembered that I had lost my old watch the year before. I was touched.

"She just *sent* you a watch out of the blue?" someone said happily. "Just like that? Man, what a girl friend!"

At that moment I could have corrected matters; I could have said who sent the watch. But it was less embarrassing to let everyone think my girl had sent it than my mother. Now I was caught in a lie and had to live with it. Very guiltily.

"Jesus, that's a beautiful stroke!" one of the veterans said. "How can you ever get ahead of a woman? What timing! Now you can't forget her, can you?"

By evening, when I was pulling KP, I was beginning to believe myself that Juanita had sent the watch. Jones is leaning back against a kitchen counter, dressed in green shorts and sandals, sipping from a hot mug of Instant Maxwell House. Lowney putters around in a loose peasant skirt and blouse without a bra, nibbling at food and directing that utensils should be carefully washed to prevent diarrhea—or "the shits," as she puts it. "You really can't blame her for sending you that watch, Johnny," she says. "She's just acting out this female thing inside her. She's powerless before it. It could be you or someone else—but the important thing is that she fills that womb soon with child."

That makes you feel great.

"What's this girl's name?" Jim demanded.

I told him, and the words sounded strange and like a betrayal.

"Do you have a picture of her?" he continued.

"Not on me." There were some of her in a bathing suit in

my wallet, and an ultimate degradation would have been to pass them around. Then possibly give a lecture on her tits, with slides.

"Christ, do I know these Southern girls," Jim twanged suddenly, screwing up his face. "They're the sweetest talking wenches in the world, but underneath as predatory as a wolf. Hell, more predatory than a wolf."

"You should know, you idiot," Lowney blasted. "Look at him. An authority now. But if I hadn't come between him and this sweet-talking woman from St. Louis, he'd be married now, like a truck driver, with twelve kids. You know what she had that stupid bastard believing? That she was a virgin, her with three kids of her own. She used to tell him, 'Ohhh, isn't it nice, Jamie, being alone by the fire like this, just the two of us? That's all I ever want in the world, just the two of us together like this.' Those letters made me vomit. You didn't know a goddam thing."

"Awwww, shit."

"No man alive is a match for a woman, I don't care who he is. Let me tell you a true story. I had Harry Handy knock me up. That man who's an alcoholic down in Robinson now. Oh, yes, I did. He was going to the University back then, a real big shot, drinking out of flasks and racing cars through Marshall. All the girls were crazy about him, and I was just a country girl, a nobody. Well, after I contrived to have him knock me up, I made him get me an abortion. Then I forced him to marry me through guilt. I really socked him to the ground, and he never knew what hit him. All women can do this—I don't care who the guy is. But what I want in this Colony are writers, not fucked-up middle-class guilt-ridden momma boys!"

*

A revolution was perhaps going on, but the seasons changed just the same. Leaves colored, and a crispness tinged the air. In October it began to be very chilly at night, and we slept under blankets and had electric heaters in our cells. Jones returned from an excursion somewhere with a terrific cold, and before long everyone came down with it in epidemic proportions. It was a blessing to stay for a day in bed—with no work at the black monster of a typewriter, no brick pile, no KP. And going to the whorehouses of Terre Haute turned out to be not the only vacation we could look forward to. Lowney's old father was running for a minor state office, and hope sprung up that the Colony crew might be dispatched to the polls in Springfield on Election Day to hand out campaign leaflets. We passed one of these leaflets around at the brick pile. It showed a picture of the old man in a shirt buttoned without tie, trying to look honest, the caption beneath reading, "The Poor Man's Friend."

"The son of a bitch is going to lose for sure," Nelms, the devotee of Hemingway, said. "Nobody wants to think of themselves as poor."

Eisenhower was running against Stevenson in the same election, and news of the campaign came to us occasionally from Lowney. "It's all over for Ike," she said, breaking gloriously into a *ramada* lunch. "They've found out Nixon's a fucking thief. Ike's probably going to have to throw him off the ticket."

The campaign seemed so farfetched that it could be happening in Austria. When we went to the barbershop and saw colored pictures in *Life* of a bald, rosy Ike and a bald, paunchy Stevenson, it triggered only a faint emotion, nothing that made you want to wolf down the text. Nothing in their lives or words remotely touched on our souls. You couldn't imagine Ike down on Cherry Street, stretched out on his back, asking for a little 'arf 'n 'arf. And Stevenson would never be caught topless in a pair of Jungle Jim britches, copying *Tender Is the Night* and rifling farts at the wall. Of course it was a little maddening, if you thought about it, that people just didn't automatically vote for Stevenson and get it over with. He was obviously the more humane and intelligent of the two. But then none of us in the Colony thought the outside world had any sense to begin with. They had to be lied to.

We did go to Springfield on Election Day to hand out leaflets, leaving in fine sunlight, a fresh soapy smell rising like steam from us, high hopes in the air. We came back in a haze of alcohol fumes and blistering oaths from Lowney and Jim, completely disorganized and defeated. The next day it was official that everyone and everything we had been for—Stevenson, Lowney's dad—had lost. We ate our raisin bread, drank our Maxwell House, and went bang on our novels as usual. The November days grew cooler yet, our fingers numbing over the typewriter keys and electric heaters glowing dryly inches away. And then the word filtered down that Lowney and Jim had decided on a winter's stay in Tucson. They would take one or two Veterans with them, and the rest of us would have to fend for ourselves somewhere. I didn't even consider going back to Tennessee; I didn't consider going anywhere.

The scenes I was pecking out now had an over-all design, and I could actually imagine a book coming out of it. Charley Henderson delivered groceries on a bicycle in a small Southern town, and knew how to play the guitar. He was under the spell of a slightly older neighbor girl, Marky, who sang and had vague aspirations toward the stage; he hero-worshiped his much older brother, Frank, who played college football and made out with all the girls. Frank, who just took off on his own from my typewriter, was finally landed by a rich man's daughter named Susan. Frank was impressed that she lived in a large white house on a hill and had great social standing in the town. Scenes popped up in a university fraternity house, in the stockroom of a grocery store, and in the backseat of an automobile. On the margin of a scene about Susan and Frank making love for the first time Lowney had written, "This is the best seduction scene I have ever read." It was a watered-down version of Juanita and myself.

The pivotal night, the night before our first actual coupling, I drove to pick Juanita up, wearing an itchy brown suit a local oil-tongued salesman had palmed off on me. It was a suit I had worn when I had traveled to Cambridge, Massachusetts, on my father's railroad pass and had tried to get in Harvard. I had tried to sneak in under the GI Bill, wanting to walk the halls that Norman Mailer, J. P. Marquand, and T. S. Eliot had. Students carried green book satchels over their shoulders, wore white bucks, and energetically handed out pamphlets about Henry Wallace in Harvard Square. The *Lampoon* was sold in every store. So different from Tennessee. The man who interviewed me had just come from the tennis court, wearing sneakers and khaki trousers and a befuddled smile. A Harvard man; he must know everything. He delightedly told me how terrible my College Boards were, as if there was art in falling so low. He asked if I had traveled all the way from Tennessee just to try to get into Harvard. I was too embarrassed to say that was the sole reason.

57

"I wanted to look around some up here too."

A silence, and someone must speak. "Are test scores all that important? Don't you judge on anything else? I've been doing a lot of reading lately."

Eh, what?

I held myself straight. "Arnold Toynbee. The works of William Shakespeare. And I peruse each issue of the *Saturday Review of Literature.*"

What was it I wanted to be in life?

"I sort of want to be a writer."

What kind?

"I was thinking about being a critic. Maybe a drama critic."

What I really wanted was to go back to Tennessee with a green book satchel, white bucks, and a sophisticated article of mine in the *Lampoon.*

"I hope you have made applications to other colleges. We only admit a thousand to Harvard each year and we have at least ten times that number of applicants. Just to be on the safe side I'd look around other places too."

I stood in the itchy brown suit that had streaks of orange running through it, thanked the man for his time, and left. . . . The rejection letter was printed with my name typed in. . . . Now, as my Plymouth bounced over the railroad tracks toward Juanita's, I told my suit it was high time it brought me some luck.

The date was our usual: a movie and then a snack at a drive-in. And it was while I had my elbows propped on a slick, formica table, looking into her blue eyes and playing with the sugar, that I spun her a yarn. It was a fantasy, an invented tale tacked onto a woman I had known briefly. Her name was Madeleine, she wore a beret, and I had lusted after her in vain during a sojourn in Quebec, Canada.

To Juanita I described how I had taken Madeleine on a canoe ride, how we had suddenly found ourselves in a shady, secluded spot, and how we had first made love. I got so far into the fantasy that I was able to picture two tiny moles on her backside and a fetching scar across her beautiful forehead. The real Madeleine had had a chunky build and a slow wit. I told about the way she would remove her beret, shake out her long chestnut hair, and then give me a sensuous, dazzling smile. I could even feel the water spray on that canoe ride and see the way the sun glinted through the tree branches. I had witnessed the real beefy Madeleine once in a wet bathing suit; her nipples had shown through ringed with long hair. To wrap up the tale I told how French-Canadian Madeleine had liked to French. That was a specialty seldom rhapsodized over by my set in Tennessee; in fact, the opposite. ("She'd suck a dick, I bet," the worst insult toward a girl.) "They call it *soixante-neuf* up there," I told Juanita. "Sixty-nine. See what it looks like when you write it down."

Something clicked behind Juanita's eyes, and her expression went soft, womanly. I had been trying to seduce her, mainly through words, for the last three months. I had never actually expected results, and therefore could have talked forever. I said, "If I could offer you marriage right now, I'd give you a bed. I can't. All I have is my car. I offer you the front and the backseat."

She nodded, the soft expression tinted with a slight flush. I knew.

We drove away, not speaking, and I came to a cutoff where we had gone once before to park and pet. "Tonight?" I said.

"Not tonight."

I called the next day and her voice was so gentle. "Come by for me at eight, darling," she said. She had started calling me, "Darling."

That night I wore my best suit, a navy blue flannel. My second-best suit was a light gray flannel. To be sporting I would wear the jacket of one suit, the trousers of the other; it gave me four suits. The navy blue with a red polka-dot tie was reserved for special evenings, my costume for this night. I sat in her living room, petting her nervous little terrier and talking to her father about Hereford cows. I didn't hear a word he said, seldom did, and jumped up when I saw her burst in in her finest silk, face glowing now in a complete flush. She kissed her father good-bye. I had never seen her do that before. He looked surprised. Then she kissed her mother. O.K., folks, tonight's the night! Couldn't they tell?

We drove off without a word and I headed for the deepest, darkest bush country I knew. It was farmland on the outskirts of town, property of an eccentric barber who had trimmed my hair many times and had once sold me a bottle of pine-tar shampoo that had brought on almost incurable dandruff. On the country road I reached over and took her hand. "I love you," I said. I had said it to her on a few other occasions, always making her mad. ("You don't! Don't say it!") I had never seen anything wrong in saying the words, everything fair in love, et cetera.

"*Do* you love me, Johnny? It is so important now. Tell me the truth."

"I do," I said quietly. "Do you love me?"

"Yes, I love you."

I cut into a gutted, rocky road that led into a jungle. To find us someone would have to wield a machete. The sickening rasp of briers scraping into the paint of my Plymouth sounded, but I headed on. A jagged tree branch tore across my window, and still I didn't stop. Only a month before I had spent fifty dollars to patch up a slightly scraped fender, but now I didn't care if the vehicle was demolished as long as we reached seclusion. Maybe we would never get out, but at least we'd have privacy tonight.

We stopped. The moon—huge and bright—shone through the foliage. I could see her face and soft expression clearly. "Let's take him out," she said. Which she did. Then: "Take everything off." I shed everything but my T-shirt. "That, too." It went, and there I was totally nude. I was thankful I'd had the presence of mind to turn the heater up. She took off her dress, carefully folding it and placing it on the backseat. Nothing hurried, nothing torn, the opposite of what I'd always pictured hot seduction to be. And there she was—everything off—moonlight draped, except for her panties. They were black and lacy. "They're the only black pair I have," she said. "I wore them especially for you."

"Take them off."

"No, darling. That's your job."

They came off easily with a little shimmy from her. Now what? Still I believed that something must surely go wrong. A beautiful girl, classical hips flanging out on the Plymouth's gray wool seat (I was saving money by not getting seat covers), her belly button there, the black forbidden triangle waiting. Could this be? She had to begin it, I was so stunned. And all the fantasies—and then some—became things I could touch, feel, smell, and hear. All the creaky sounds from the car, the slur and slup of love, the words that caressed my ears and those that sprang unbidden from my throat. "Do you like it fast like this? Or slow—like this?"

61

"Just the way you do it, darling. Just the way you do."

Could that be her lovely black head down there? Could this actually, truly be Juanita throwing her knees gracefully apart and sinking down astride me? Good-bye everything that Kinsey wrote. Farewell Krafft-Ebing and Havelock Ellis. All the barnyard gossip I had ever heard had missed the mark; all the movies, all the books, all the sermons from the pulpit. Only one thing caused a little worry to click away well back in my mind. Her alacrity. How could she immediately spring into such intricate positions? How did she know how to do it? Was she being an actress here too, acting out tales that had been told her? Once we went to a Catholic mass—her first time—and she had genuflected and crossed herself and made the Holy Water fly. She even lit a candle. She was more Catholic than the Catholics.

Later, after our lovemaking, she said, "It's because of you that I can do those things. You bring them out of me, you wonderful lover you."

Now, defying physics, I'm sitting back on the car seat and she's coupled to me from above. Hard thrusts send her head against the ceiling. Gentle swayings allow looks in the eye and whole-mouth kisses. I'm into her in as many places as I can find. By arching her back she can place one breast, then the other, in my fishlike mouth. "Darling, come," she says. How does she know words like come? "Come in me."

"We don't want to make a baby."

"We won't. My period starts in a few days. I've timed this."

The magic word—period. Everything has worked so perfectly that I guard against wrecking it at the end. I come, almost politely, the first time I have done so in a woman without a shield of latex around me—a few times in Korea using

62

two rubbers at once, the fear of Oriental clap so strong. Now we put on our clothes, looking into each other's eyes in wonder. We light one cigarette and pass it back and forth. The car scrapes and spins from the bush, and I drive slowly toward town, Juanita close beside me and putting on fresh lipstick. The wonder of girls. The wonder of love. In a drive-in Juanita gets a lemonade and cherry pie. I tip the country-girl curbhop fifty cents, the biggest tip I've ever left. I look over at Juanita. She is sitting far down in the seat, back against the door, drawing on a straw. A flush comes again over her. That mouth now with lipstick, those legs now enclosed in stockings, those breasts covered by padded bra. I know how they are naked and always will. Later that night, alone in the old bathroom at home, I take out my dick and look at it in disbelief. You actually went up inside her. Imagine that. Wow!

The great things in life have only just begun!

Part Two

And so came the late fall day when Lowney called me to her bungalow. Her hair, I noticed, was almost iron gray, less dark than when I'd first come that summer. She started off by asking if I'd like a drink. It was highly unusual to be offered a drink of whisky at the Colony, and I declined for fear a delicate balance between us would be broken. Then my book wouldn't get written and I would never become famous enough to make love to Debbie Reynolds. I didn't want to dwell on it, but it did cross my mind that Lowney might have considered the two of us making love. With *Lowney?* How could our relationship—cemented by my total fear of her—continue after that?

If I didn't want a drink, she continued, then how about a mug of Instant Maxwell House?

We sat facing each other, swigging on coffee and me flicking cigarette ash into my Levi cuffs because I couldn't find an ashtray. Lowney did not smoke.

"John, I'm not going to let George stay here at the Colony this winter. God knows what he might do to Mrs. Handy. What I need is someone who is steady and that I can depend upon. I've already asked Jud. He's . . . writing . . . he's going to write one hell of a good book once he gets those fucking cobwebs out of his brain. I want the two of you to stay with Mrs. Handy in her house, keep an eye on things. That's all you have to do. Only don't let that old babe screw you up or turn you against me. Oh, she'd love to, but don't let her. If you knew what she's done to Harry Handy, you still wouldn't believe it. I think you and Jud can run things fine. Now do you want to stay over this winter or do you have to go back to Tennessee?"

"I'll stay."

Jud wore smudged glasses with colorless frames. His hair was falling out, and he had large, dirty brown teeth that were nearly constantly clamped down on a well-used pipe. He moved slowly, methodically, often with a bemused smile on his face, and before uttering a word he always cleared his throat a few times. He never had much to say. I found him lying back in his room that smelled heavily of sweaty clothing and pipe tobacco, reading. I told him what Lowney had proposed, and asked what he thought. He cleared his throat several times.

68

"I think we'll get along fine," he said softly. "We should get a lot of writing done."

A swivel-necked lamp glowed on a stand behind his head, washing his bemused face and smudged glasses in brilliant, third-degree light. The book he had been reading lay open across his chest, and soon he was reaching on his side for a match to relight his pipe. Our conversation was the longest I had ever had with him. Of all the people in the Colony, I knew Jud the least.

Perc shipped out as a merchant seaman that winter. George packed his belongings in boxes tied up with rope, put on a clean shirt, and took a bus back to his hometown in Ohio. Nelms, the good-natured man with a hairy chest and a devotion to Hemingway, took a factory job in Bloomington, Indiana. Bayard was hanging out at coffee shops and beer joints in Robinson, and doing errands for his mother. Los Angeles and San Francisco and Washington, D.C., were touted as good spots for quick jobs and fast exits. I often looked up from my typewriter, imagining a rented room swept by sea breezes in Los Angeles, at night a whole horde of actresses and other stunning creatures out there waiting, all seeking romance and a bed partner. But I was going nowhere.

On a sunny fall afternoon I helped Jones batten down objects within his silver trailer. Squatting on the thin floor near him, I caught great martini whiffs as he explained what should be done. He had been through this many times before, but occasionally now in a welter of alcohol fumes he forgot where certain bolts should be fastened. We secured his typewriter, his unabridged dictionary, and the cups he drank from, and I felt honored to be connected so intimately with such a great author. Then the Tucson-bound caravan rolled away, leaving sad empty spaces behind. "You're in charge now, Johnny," Lowney said. "Do as much work as you can, and let me know if you have any trouble. It should be very quiet here, though. Good-bye! Good-bye!"

"So long . . . so long!"

That evening Jud and I dressed up, and I drove both of us to Terre Haute in the Plymouth. Here was real freedom at last, better than the sporadic night out during the summer Colony days. We swung down the big-city streets and drank in cheap joints. We could go to a movie, eat greasy food, and possibly we could pick up a couple of nice girls somewhere with the thought of later assignations in the coming winter season. And there was always the whorehouse. Here was freedom, the kind that stretched out before you for months. Jud must have shared these thoughts with me, for his bemused smile became plastered on. Quite frequently he left his drink to wander to a joint's rest room. These strolls began to seem a little peculiar. "You got bad kidneys, Jud?"

"Nooo," and he opened his jacket to reveal a pint of liquor he kept stashed in an inside pocket. Carrying his own stuff that way, he only had to buy one drink for show in the joint. It was a trick that I knew something about from life in Tennessee. Jud's smile broadened into a slow, silent chuckle. He was not exactly the best drinking companion in the world.

"I think we've got a pretty good deal this winter," I said, having made the same statement several times before that evening. I really had little to say to him, and racked my brains for new ideas. The conversation finally fell dead, and only the thought of my new freedom kept me perked up. Then, with no warning and no throat clearing, Jud jumped into a strange line of thought: "Have you ever fucked a woman in her seventies or eighties?"

70

"Uh—no."

"Guys"—lighting his pipe, sucking on it—"lots of guys miss out on the best stuff in the world by not knowing what's good. I came down"—clearing his throat now, staring into space—"once from my room and caught my landlady taking a bath. You couldn't believe this creamy white skin she had and that gray hair floating out on her shoulders. Those kind of women can take care of a man right. I used to watch my mother bathe too, when my father was out working in the day. I hated my bastard of a father. We got in some terrible fights. I wanted to kill him."

"Yeah? Jesus."

"I'm going to try and find me an old woman tonight, and fuck her. You don't have to pay them, either. Lots of times they pay you."

"I like them a little younger."

"You don't know what's good."

Later on he did strike up a conversation with a hefty, heavily rouged, booze-soddened woman who looked well past sixty. She had friends with her and couldn't leave with Jud. But she gave him her name and number, and he took it down carefully. "I'm going to get me some of that stuff next week," he said.

Before the midnight drive back, I stopped in a filling station and ordered two dollars' worth of gas. I waited for Jud to offer a dollar toward the cost of travel, but he didn't budge, gazing dreamily in front of himself. Perhaps he was thinking about the elderly woman. I cleared my throat. "Jud, do you think you could spare a buck toward the ride?"

"Noooo"—with his ironic, goofy smile.

In the old gabled house we arose before sunup every morning, keeping Colony hours. Jud would creak open my

71

door in the front, downstairs bedroom, clear his throat, and murmur, "Uh—John, a little before six." He owned an alarm clock; I did not. In the well-cleaned kitchen, where the old-timey electric stove, toaster, and refrigerator seemed props for a 1918 advertisement, Mrs. Handy would be darting around with the lightness of a feather. We took our coffee and toast quietly, our eyes still puffed from sleep, not really having a thing to say to one another. Increasingly I suffered an intensely empty feeling when I awoke in the morning. I imagined how a warm, snug body might feel beside me, and I could almost miraculously discern an interminable future of waking alone in beds far from home.

The pages in my manuscript grew at the rate of three or four new ones a day. I would pry myself away from sex fantasies, type a few sentences or paragraphs, and then think of excuses to get me away from the black monster. I waited for the sound of the mailman at a little past nine. The Chicago *Tribune* arrived, and that was always good for a fifteen- or twenty-minute break. If I had a particularly good run at the typewriter—say, a page and a half at one spurt—I would reward myself with a short walk. Strolling down a narrow road, I thought of the characters and situations I had just put on paper, their reality stronger than memories from the actual past. Most often the characters moved unbidden through remembered settings—a grocery store I had worked in, a neighbor's house, my own house. Juanita worked her way into all of the female characters, brassy, adventurous, loving. My male characters were all frustrated in the search for fame and glory.

At noon the Handy household ceased creation. We took turns preparing meals for each other, simple Colony fare such as boiled potatoes, poached eggs, and large-curd cottage cheese. We made bright small talk at the table. As an economy measure Mrs. Handy kept heat at a minimum in the old drafty house and the water tap marked "Hot" never rose above a tepid state. Just a few inches of bath water could be drawn in the chilly bathroom before it lost its hint of warmness. In the afternoons I stalked the streets of Marshall, swigging an occasional ten-cent glass of beer, watching action in a poolroom, and longing for one of the neat, pretty cheerleader-types who hung out in a popular drugstore. One would be dressed in a pleated skirt, fluffy tight sweater with a gold basketball bouncing between her breasts, and acting bored and superior the way Juanita could affect so well. Now and then I started passing Jud coming down the street in the opposite direction, and we only gave each other the barest of nods. In late wintry afternoons he began digging up forgotten carrots and turnips from the Colony garden, and placing them in use for the evening meal. He wrote frequently in the afternoons, and he attended every change of picture at the one cramped movie house in town.

The noon hour was approaching, and I sat behind the black monster waiting for the reprieve of lunch. Instead the phone rang near Mrs. Handy's room in the back, and she came to my door. "Somebody wants you," she said.

I held the receiver, and noticed that Mrs. Handy had not gone back to her typing, nor were creative sounds coming from Jud's room above. It was Juanita on the line, long distance. "Have you forgotten me, darling?" How high, girlish the voice. How innocent and sweet it sounded. Jesus, how much I had missed it.

"No, baby, how could I ever forget you?"

"Then, listen, I'm going to fly up and see you. I can be there this weekend. I must see you. It can't end like this."

My mind jumped into the consequences. Lowney would learn of it. She would stop considering me a writer, the Fastest Learner. I wouldn't have fame and glory. The idea of meeting a plane and securing a hotel room was enervating. And this weekend was my time to cook, I remembered. "Baby, baby. I'm going to come home Christmas. That's only a few weeks. I'll see you then. We'll talk over everything. We must be able to work this out because I do love you."

"Do you, Johnny?"

"I do, I do."

"And I love you. I'll wait, I'll wait."

Eating cottage cheese at lunch that day, I held in a bright happy laugh that threatened to break out of me. We would see each other in a few weeks. I was being allowed to keep writing my novel, and she would always be waiting. It was having your cake and eating it too. Mrs. Handy and Jud curiously watched me, as if they had had a tap on the phone.

Came a crisp cold morning, and I pulled the Plymouth out of the garage for the drive to Tennessee for the holidays. Again freedom, this time from Jud and Mrs. Handy and up each morning before dawn. I drove straight, a sixteen-hour trip, savoring the quiet expectant moments alone in a car. Once home, I had a hot bath, slept in a huge bed between clean sheets, and ate tremendous Southern meals cooked by my mother. I looked up some old drinking buddies, answered endless questions my father put to me, and walked familiar streets. Steeling myself on an afternoon, I called Juanita where she had a part-time job. My voice came out harsh, and I heard a slight gasp from her. "I'll be by to pick you up," I said. "We'll talk."

She looked so forlorn as she stepped from the store, a purse in her hand, wearing some flat-heeled shoes she had bought

74

since I last saw her. She seemed to have grown an inch or two taller. Her hair was a little longer. We drove in silence for a moment, and then she said, "I think I'll kiss you. I haven't kissed you yet." Then: "Do you still love me?"

"No," I heard myself say. I hadn't planned to say it; it just came forth like a character in the book I was writing. "I don't love you anymore."

I drove the Plymouth over a road we had taken often for lovemaking sessions. Here we came bouncing over railroad tracks; there was the junkyard to the right; up ahead was Langston High School, the Negro school. Some color left her face, she wet her lips, and then she began to cry. The moment was over in a second, but it's never ceased playing in my mind. In the car I slouched down and didn't take my eyes from the road. She kissed me wetly on the cheek. "This is so hard," I said. "I'm only human. Maybe we shouldn't kiss and play around. It's so unfair to you. It's not right."

She got out slowly at her home, slower than Mrs. Handy. "I'll see you again before I go back," I said, feeling it was a lie. "Good-bye."

"Good-bye."

I inched the car forward, and she stood there on the pavement. If it had been in the style of the movies we had grown up with, that would have been our final moment: her standing there, my driving away at a snail's pace, *finis*. But, lo and behold, the very next night I got drunk at a friend's, called her to come pick me up, and told her I loved her and loved her and loved her.

She drove us to a drive-in movie. Nudged in a stall, a flickering, unwatched Ma and Pa Kettle in front of us, I took off her sweater and brassiere and licked her back. What would Lowney say to that? Did sex manuals or James Jones

75

novels ever go into the licking of a bare back? It tasted salty. When she finally raised those greenish blue eyes, she asked again, "Do you love me, Johnny?"

"Yes, I do." I was afraid she would stop.

But she didn't stop, and I didn't either. Steam rose to seal the windows, and our lovemaking resumed where it had left off before I signed on at the Handy Colony. "Forget worry over the novel," I told myself. "Try to forget that Lowney might object to this visit home." Making love to Juanita was returning to a familiar language after a long stay among exotic, foreign-speaking people. But I was different now, a Veteran. How could I really explain to Juanita about copying Faulkner and not catching any news and the summer of going once every great while into Terre Haute to pound away at a whore? Could she ever appreciate Lowney's mania for enemas, Jell-o, and the Masters of the Far East? Must she think I'm crazy now to spend a winter with a ninety-year-old woman and a balding man who constantly cleared his throat? It was better not to go into it.

"Marry me, Johnny, before you go back. We don't have to tell anyone. It can be our secret, and you can still stay up there as long as you have to."

"We can't do that. That wouldn't work. It would make matters worse."

"But what am I going to do? I can't live the way it's been."

"We used to have such fun together, didn't we?"

Up at the Handy Colony meant Freedom, Possibilities, Writing the Book; down here in Tennessee meant Marriage, Babies, and Responsibilities. Or that had been the way Lowney had presented the case. Over and over and over.

Juanita and I saw each other through the rest of the holidays. She cooked me a meal when her parents were away on a short visit, and cried when I couldn't eat all of the pork chops. We were wetly connected once as we heard her father wheel his big car into the garage, and I ran around the bedroom, stuffing things in and trying to engrave an innocent, lazy look on my face. The father came in chortling like Santa Claus, while the mother stayed a few paces behind and quietly went through the Southern-type amenities. While I threw my butt out so the lingering thrust of an erection wouldn't show, I talked the required period to her father. When I had talked to him before, I could easily chat about the weather and Hereford cows. Now the talk became difficult. He didn't seem to quite grasp where I had been. Somehow the notion of my being at a Colony struck him as slightly off-color, something that must not be spoken about directly. For a moment I thought he had confused a Writing Colony with a Nudist Colony—and I'm still not really sure. As he plowed into the subject of the downtown Christmas decorations, as sponsored by the Chamber of Commerce, I looked him in the eye and said to myself, "Sir, five minutes before you strutted in here I had my dick in your daughter. Now I stand here calmly, my butt sticking out so my late hard-on will not show, and I seem for all the world to be enraptured over your sterling insights into Christmas decorations. Things are never what they seem. Never, ever."

There were a few more times with Juanita during that Christmas season. There was a movie we forced ourselves to watch; there were tears, forlorn conversations, and sad partings at her door. Then came the final good-bye from my car. "We'll work something out," I said, confused once more. "Please quit being so blue."

"I'll try. Maybe I shouldn't have held you so tightly. By

gosh, I know I shouldn't have let you make me. If you hadn't laid me yet, you'd want to marry me."

"It's not that; truly it's not that."

"Somebody wants to introduce me to this guy. He's supposed to be rich or something. I guess"—sighing—"I might as well go out with him."

Lowney had told me about this strategy; Juanita was trying to make me jealous. "Go out with him then. We should both stop thinking so much about each other. It's crippling us."

"I'll try. Good-bye, John."

"Good-bye, Juanita."

*

The drive back to Illinois took place in gray, damp weather. I stopped in starkly lit diners with grizzled men in greasy caps who sat at counters and picked their teeth. Sad-looking tinsel from the recent Christmas season whipped in the breeze as I drove through one coal-mining town after another. Dejected, stoop-shouldered women lethargically pushed battered baby carriages, and old men lounged on street corners chewing tobacco and spitting to the side. Everything gritty and grimy and infinitely bleak. I was heading through this for the reward of a Victorian house and an unfinished book that only Lowney and I had seen. (Or Jud, who may have slipped into my room during my absence.) Behind me I had left the only woman I would ever love quite so uninhibitively and confidently.

> I should have been a pair of ragged claws
> Scuttling across the floors of silent seas.

O scorned T.S., how well you put it, baby!

*

It got so that I could not bear the sight of Jud. There he was at breakfast, drinking tea from a teapot and sucking through bubbling spit on his pipe, his large teeth brown and uneven and decaying. Here he would be going in slow motion up the stairs, or settling with a squirm into a chair, or poking through the rooms. He carried a faint, baffled grin on his face, and his voice (after the usual overhaul of the throat) came out quietly with hints of menace like the mad-scientist voice of Boris Karloff in an old Warner's film. I saw him at breakfast, lunch, and dinner—and I became quite familiar with his favorite dishes ("I got a hankering for corned beef.") and his complete repertoire of table manners. He crossed his legs and jiggled his foot in lingering after the meal, spilling pipe ashes over the front of his soiled T-shirt and then whacking them off toward the party beside him. A bitter aroma of Prince Albert soon combined with Mrs. Handy's powdery scent in the kitchen.

When I drove off in my car for an afternoon excursion—always with the hope of somehow meeting a fresh girl—I felt guilty if I left Jud behind. Every time I asked if he'd like to join me, he accepted with a smiling nod. Once, in answering a deep unarticulated need, I flew into a college cafeteria in Terre Haute, striking up a spirited conversation with a co-ed who had corn-silk hair. She was about to accept the offer of taking a walk and hearing about the glories of novel writing when she spied a balding man with pipe leaning on a door-jamb and gazing our way.

"Who's that?"

79

"A friend of mine. A writer. Do you have a girl friend you could fix him up with?"

The girl with the corn-silk hair did not leave the cafeteria with me that day; she would not give me her telephone number. Jud and I went off to have some beers together, where he told me about an elderly, gray-haired woman he hoped to visit soon in a nearby town. "She's dying for it," he said, "although she hasn't said it. You can tell."

A youth who had been with us in the summer now attended an upstate teacher's college, and he invited me up one Saturday for relaxation and old times' sake. "Lots of girls here." I halfheartedly asked Jud if he'd like to come along, and he accepted with alacrity. The college man, who was a dance-band musician as well as a would-be writer, had an offhand, unassumed familiarity with girls, and he easily arranged dates for us. Jud's girl had dark eyes, pale skin, and a plump build, and the two of them sat in the Plymouth's backseat. I drove beside a bubbly, very pretty girl, who didn't seem to take anything seriously and who didn't seem too bright. Just my type. As we neared a roadhouse where we were to meet our Colony comrade, Jud's dark-haired date reached over and whispered something in my date's ear. "Could you pull in this filling station?" my bubbly friend said. "We must go to the little girls' room."

When the girls were out of earshot, I whispered to Jud, "How you getting along?"

"Uhhh—fine," he said.

The girls came back to the car looking glum. "We've got to go back to the dorm," the bubbly one said. "Fran's just remembered that she has a test early Monday and has to study for it tonight."

"A *test!* That's ridiculous."

No amount of coaxing could get her to change her mind. Fran must return to the dorm. She was sorry, but that was the way it was. The bubbly one said at first she would stay with Jud and me, but after some swift, dark looks from her friend, changed her mind. She would stay with her friend in the dorm; her friend needed company. She was sorry, but that was the way it was. After dropping the girls off, Jud continued sitting in the backseat and I chauffeured him to the roadhouse. "What in God's name did you say or do to that girl?" I said.

"Nothing. She wasn't my type."

We spent the evening with our Colony comrade in the roadhouse, getting sloshed on bourbon and Coke. Later on—after the roadhouse closed and our comrade had dropped off his own date—we ended up in spare dormitory bunks. "I wonder what the hell you could have said to Fran," our comrade said to Jud. "I know you couldn't have *shown* her anything new because she was gangbanged by the whole football team last weekend."

The next day, mortally hung over, I began the long drive back to Marshall by first pulling in at the inevitable filling station. "Uh—Jud, couldn't you spare just a little on the gas? Even a buck would help. I don't have any income either, you know."

He cleared his throat, but didn't say a word.

Back in the daily grind, I got three letters from Juanita. They came a week apart, and were like a prizefighter's punches: a left jab, a right cross, and then a straight blow to the heart. The first letter thanked me for being with her during the Christmas season. ("You wonderful you, I wish I had you here to kiss now.") I wrote her, telling her in five pages how much I loved her, but I was physically unable to mail

81

the letter. Her second letter was a wild plea, and I thought I found tear stains on it. ("Help me, help me! What terrible wrong have I done to deserve this? Why are you making me go through this hell on earth? Can't you even write me a letter? Oh, God, help me.")

I paled, and immediately wrote page after page, telling her that whatever she wished was all right now by me. I loved her deeply; I always would. I couldn't bear her being so unhappy. But I got so carried away by the composition of the letter, so rhapsodic over my own sentiments, that I was still writing it when her third and final letter arrived. It had no salutation, and it ended, "I have torn up all of your letters and pictures. There is nothing of you that remains with me now except in memory, and I shall do my best to rid myself of that. I never want to see your face or hear your voice or read a line you ever write again. I do not want your name spoken in my presence. I hope your soul rots in hell."

She had once made me feel like a king; she had truly first given me my manhood. Now I never had felt as low and miserable and worthless in my life.

In the afternoons I took long, exhausting walks, looking with dazed eyes into the warm-glowing windows of family homes, into department stores where staples for housewives were on display, and into smoky, cramped beer joints where lonely men whiled away their time. Moving like a zombie toward our Victorian house one day, I watched tiny Mrs. Handy, with an egg basket in the crook of her arm, begin to cross the highway. With a brief, stiff jerk of her head, she scanned the distance and took little, toes-in steps across the expanse of highway concrete. She wore heavy cotton stockings over legs no larger than the grip-end of a baseball bat, and her hips were as narrow as a pre-adolescent boy's. She wasn't wearing her glasses. As she stepped past the highway's black dividing line, I witnessed a trailer truck come hurtling around the bend and down the slight hill. It was roaring. My mouth began working, but no sound came out. If I yelled, something told me right away, she would stop dead in her tracks to await the impact of the truck. With my hands at my temples, I watched her step full into the truck's path, then a few feet from instant death start a fantastic toes-in sprint like a chicken scurrying away from the farmer's ax. The truck missed her by possibly two and a half inches, no horn blast or grind of brakes from the driver. Perhaps she had been too small for him to see from his high perch. She continued her journey on the other side of the highway, the egg basket in her arm.

Jud came and went from my path, with a coloring of the face and a rumble from the throat. I passed him on the street, hardly slowing down. Lying on my bed in semidarkness and despair, I could hear his slow steps going up the stairs, and then a salute of typing from his second-story room. I was learning far more about him than I wanted to know. For instance, he made no sound when he took a bath, and his ankles had a tendency to swell and turn purplish. I took my car out for spins alone, to hell with him!, playing the radio as I used to do with Juanita beside me. At the dining table we talked of strange birds we had seen in the side yard, of the lengthening of the days and how spring was on the way, and about incidents that had happened to us in Kroger's while shopping. Mrs. Handy sat as a buffer between Jud and myself.

I was washing the dishes, Jud was drying, and Mrs. Handy had wandered away, since she wasn't on KP that day. Jud had rolled up his sleeves, displaying large, tanned biceps, and he considered each plate a moment before drying it in a

83

slow circular motion. All at once he put down a plate, the drying cloth neatly beside it, and came to within a few inches of me. The machine-gun blast of his voice was without a stutter or stumble, his face turning the purplish color of his swollen ankles, and it was so unlike what I expected from him that I couldn't take in the words at first. Only a minute before he had been clearing his throat and talking about turnips from the garden. " . . . *someday I'm going out and smash that car*," he was bellowing, fist up in my face, *"and then I'm going to come in and smash you!"*

"Take it easy, Jud," I was saying—my turn to speak very softly. "Take it easy, please. What's wrong with you? What's happened?"

Like Spencer Tracy's hairy Mr. Hyde turning by degrees back into serene Dr. Jekyll, Jud began changing gradually from purplish-faced fury back into his gray shell. He finished drying the plates, leisurely putting them away. In my room I could still see his fist with the knuckles turning white, could still feel the lash of his words on my cheeks, and could still picture the depth of hate within his yellowish cat eyes. Could we keep on living under the same roof? I couldn't go back to Tennessee. Where could I go? My book was growing now; I was doing what Lowney told me to do. In late afternoon I climbed the stairs, knocked at Jud's door, and then heard a throat-clearing and a gentle, "Come in."

I sat hunched forward in a straight-back chair while he lay in bed with a wreath of stale pipe smoke above him and a book on his T-shirted chest. He waited for me to speak, an amused, indulgent grin on his face. A shit-eating grin.

"Jud, I don't know what's happened, but I'm sorry," I said, debasing myself. "The car is out there in the garage, and it's as much yours as mine. I don't know what's happened"—repeating, repeating—"but I'm sorry. We've got to be able to get along together here. I'll do the very best I can. Is that O.K.? Are we still friends?"

He cleared his throat, nodded, and drew on his pipe. A hot, wild glow shone in his eyes.

In my book I wrote about Frank Henderson, the older brother, getting married and hating the small-town job he found himself in. Charley ambled along, observing what was going on, passive, vaguely frustrated, but not knowing what to do about it. I had him play the guitar a lot. There was a fight between Frank and some Negroes that suddenly began writing itself one day. Frank and Charley were out driving when a carload of blacks nearly sideswiped them, causing Frank to chase them down and start a knife and fistfight. With car headlights illuminating a secluded expanse near some woods, Frank cursed the Negroes, fought wildly, and soon had the point of a pigsticker on a black man's Adam's apple. "Don't, please, Frank," Charley pleaded from the sidelines.

"Don't kill me, man," the Negro moaned. "I'm sorry I near sideswiped you. Forgive me, man."

"I should stick this through to the ground, you son of a bitch," Frank said. Negro girls wailed in the background, wringing their hands and praying to God. Then, as abruptly as it had begun, Frank tossed the knife away and left the Negroes in peace. Fights and near fights were forever cropping up in my manuscript. Charley would be sitting in Sunday school or later getting drunk in college, and all at once a hothead would barge up in a fighting stance. There came equal amounts of blind aggression and abject cowardice.

And then Bayard drove up from Robinson in real life with some news that came as a godsend. Jim and Lowney had called and wanted Bayard and me to make it out to Tucson as soon as possible. I was to stop writing for the moment (God, how that came as a relief!), and follow what Bayard told me. Lowney had sent a hundred dollars for traveling expenses, but we weren't going to go by bus. Hitchhike? Take my Plymouth? No, Bayard now had a divorcee girl friend in Robinson with two small kids, and she would drive us to El Paso where her ex-in-laws now lived. The kids could visit their relatives. She would have company. We would pay for the gas, a minor sum. Then Bayard and I could take the bus from El Paso to Tucson, and have money left out of the traveling expenses. But why did Lowney and Jim want us in Tucson? They wouldn't ever want us just for *us*.

"Well," Bayard drawled, "Jim wants us to ride two motorcycles back here to the Colony. He's got 'em on his hands, and it costs a hell of a lot to ship 'em by railway express. This way it don't cost him much."

"Look, I've only been on a motorcycle once. That time on Old Blue. But I don't give a shit if I get killed just as long as I get out of here for a while. Yipeeee!"

"Listen, you can practice a little bit out in Tucson on the sly before we take 'em on the highway. There's nothing to it. I told Jim and Lowney you was an expert now and I've got 'em believing it. Just keep quiet out there about your recent riding experience. Anything else?"

"When do we roll?"

"Tomorrow. You'll stay at my house down in Robinson tonight. We'll get an early start."

*

It was a Ford convertible with rips in its canvas top. Bayard

86

and I had been drinking beer since getting together the night before, and as we drove toward the highway pointing west, in late afternoon, we carried several six-packs of warm beer by our feet.

Abigail sat between us. She was a thin, vaguely pretty girl with hair out of place and a cigarette going nearly constantly. In the backseat Abigail's two boys, no bigger than fireplugs, alternately fought and played games together. Jimmy, the older one, had a wise, tight streetface, choosing the games and winning the fights. Joey was plump, easy to cry, and liked to sit on people's laps. In the front seat we passed beer around, smoked continually, and watched the scenery change—Abigail in the center and Bayard and I taking turns driving.

"You kids cut the fighting out," Abigail would bark suddenly, wheeling around and aiming an openhanded smack. "We have a lot of miles to go and I'm not going to spend my time separating you two."

An out-of-sight kick from Jimmy to his brother; a scream from Joey.

"All right, all right, I WARNED YOU!" And Abigail's palm went to work on both of them. Only Joey cried. Jimmy's face got tighter, more withdrawn. Joey wanted his neck hugged.

"Listen, you kids," Bayard said, removing a beer can from his lips. "I'm going to lay into both of you unless you pipe down. You got that?" A wink to me, and *sotto voce:* "Do I scare 'em or do I not?"

We passed through St. Louis, which was full of stoplights, glittering streetcar tracks, and that unmistakable, big-city bustle. The Mississippi River was a grayish, muddy color, and didn't seem as wide as it should be. "Here I am," I kept telling myself, "going across the river that Mark Twain wrote about."

Ahead of us at a toll booth a low-slung, snappy car with a crowd of Negroes inside drove up, and at the decisive moment for turning over change the driver slapped the hand of the groggy attendant and sped away in cackles and plumes of exhaust. No one chased them. We paid the toll, careful to have our beer well hidden. And then onward—through darkening skies and finally the night—winding around mountain curves and stopping only when the boys in the back demanded for the hundreth time that they be allowed to pee.

"You just went twenty-five miles back!" Abigail said, the cigarette jiggling between her lips. "Now you can just hold it for a while."

"I can't, Momma, I can't!"

"I'm going to slap both of you good in a few minutes. You just want attention. Now you hold it!"

After dinner in a cavernous resort-type restaurant that only had us for customers, Jimmy, the slimmer one, fit himself into the shelf above the backseat and went to sleep. Joey took the whole backseat. In the front I made the mistake (as usual) of coming on too strong too soon with Abigail. I rattled off some of the old standard words, spoke offhandedly about secret things, and thought I was worldly wise. After all, didn't we use those words all the time at the Colony, and wasn't I an artist? Abigail fumbled a cigarette in and out of her mouth and declined an offer of a beer. Maybe, I thought, she wishes she had Bayard to herself and begrudges me space in the car. Forever the politican, I stopped the Anglo-Saxon words and know-it-all comments and started on non-talk: the best kind of house in which to raise children, the way teenagers are different today than yesterday, and what kind of girls make the best wives. At the wheel, Bayard sipped beer and kept the gas near the floorboard. We had decided to keep going all night, and not stop in a motel.

A misty rain fell as we came down from the Ozarks, and then it lifted as we drove through a medium-sized town that was quietly asleep. Lush trees lined the well-cared-for streets, and dewdrops of rain stood out on the branches in the glow of frequently spaced streetlamps. There was a hot-rod jalopy some kid was fixing up and had parked importantly in a driveway. There were long green lawns, basketball hoops above garage doors, and oval drinking fountains on the grounds for birds. I thought about what life might be like, living in this sleeping town with Juanita. She would have kids, I would drive up after work in late afternoons, and there would be plenty of space and freedom for lovemaking. . . .

We left the town. We cut into the edge of Kansas—roads, markings, billboards changing as if going into a foreign country—and Abigail takes the wheel of her own car for the first time. A cigarette bobbing up and down in her mouth, one of her kids suddenly whining, so she has to reach around and smack or caress, Abigail drives into Oklahoma as rain comes down again. It starts in little spirals on the windshield and changes into grayish lashes that weave in the headlights like snow. Water falls through the holes in the convertible top and the wipers turn in a wet flop-flop fashion. Vision is soon down to that in a strong fog. Still, Abigail chatters about what makes a good wife, racing the motor one moment, putting on the brake the next. Suddenly, the side of a bridge looms up through the sheets of rain. Bayard, who has been dozing, sits bolt upright. I touch Abigail's cigarette hand in midair.

"Stop, baby. Maybe someone else should take the wheel."

She stops almost diagonally in the highway, the car's hood pointing toward the bridge abutment. "But my turn's only been a short while. I'm not the least bit tired."

"It's this rain, Abigail. You're not accustomed to driving in a rainstorm like this."

Bayard takes the wheel, crawling over us to get to it. Almost immediately the rain stops, the moon comes out, and we pass by dark, ominous oil derricks. Bayard goes back to sipping a can of beer while speeding along, and I find myself nodding with sleep. But I don't want to lose consciousness for fear a wreck will happen then. I reason that if I am awake, I can somehow prevent it. Suddenly, while I nod, there is a screech of brakes, then another long one, and finally a head-jerking stop. The car is nearly diagonal with the highway again. Bayard puts the gear in reverse and goes back down the highway. A Westerner in a sharp blue outfit—with much silver and curlicues of white thread—stands by the road. On his head is the tallest, whitest cowboy hat I have ever seen. "Need a lift, buddy?" Bayard says. He is always doing the unexpected.

"Mighty kind of you. My car broke down bout a half-mile back. I'm trying to get to a garage. Sure you got room in there?"

"We'll make room," Bayard says. "Hop right in."

The boys in the back wake up and begin rubbing their eyes. The cowboy sits half on me and half on Abigail. Bayard offers him a beer, which he declines. His hat keeps bumping against the convertible top as he tries to keep his balance through Bayard's breakneck speed. We ask him if people here in the West wear his kind of suit all the time. "This is a kind of dress suit," he says. "You wouldn't wear it to work."

90

We want to know if he rides horses and shoots guns and brands cattle. He does. "You're the first cowboy we've seen this trip," we tell him over and over. "Just a few hours ago we were driving through towns with smokestacks and going across the Mississippi." After we drop him off in front of an all-night garage, we wonder what he thinks of us. Surely we were just as strange a sight to him as he was to us. Two men and a woman swigging beer in the front seat of a dilapidated convertible while two sleep-ridden kids moaned in the back. Could he have appreciated the fact that Bayard and I were off to see the great Jim Jones and return East on motorcycles?

In the gray light of the new day we witness something new in our journey. Sagebrush as large as Christmas trees is flying across the highway in a strong, galelike wind. The unfamiliar plant skips up and down, like an airplane landing, disappearing over flat, patchy land. In the distance, here and there, a few wind-whipped cattle huddle together and look miserable. It is the most forlorn, depressing stretch of earth I have ever seen, and I had been over the dusty terrain between Yong Dong Po and Seoul, Korea. It is the Texas Panhandle.

A mood of dejection hits us all—even the boys in the back who were coming awake—and Bayard becomes incensed over a behemoth, diesel-spewing monster directly in front of us now. He starts swinging around it, but there is the crest of a hill ahead. There is little traffic, so the odds are good that nothing is coming our way—but we do not know for sure.

"I'm going to take a chance," Bayard drawls. "See you in hell if we lose."

"Don't do it, Bayard," I say. "Wait till after the hill. Come on now."

"Bayard, now don't you do it," Abigail says. "Why take such a chance."

"The son of a bitch is bothering me, that's why." His knuckles turn white on the steering wheel, but he doesn't jam the gas to the floorboard. He waits until we get over the hill (no car was coming), and then flies around the truck like sagebrush. I let out my breath and swig on beer. It would have been instant, violent death *if* a car had been coming and *if* Bayard had tried to take the truck sooner. What would my parents have thought about such a death in the Panhandle? Could it ever be explained in funeral services at the Central Baptist Church? Would Juanita have known the real truth, whatever it was? Would she have thought I had stopped loving her before my death?

We eat ham and eggs with grits on the side in a starkly lit cafe. The waitress is a blonde, a few sizes too large for her white uniform, and she speaks with more of a twang and drawl than I had heard since leaving Tennessee. Other early morning customers hunch over their coffee, very slow moving and not talkative. The ever-present Panhandle wind rattles the front window, which is frosted with fine yellowish dust. It is not a happy place, and we do not linger over coffee. Stopping in a beer joint in Amarillo to pee, I note this verse parallel to my eyes:

> If a Texan's brains were as big as his balls,
> There'd be no writing on the shithouse walls.

We drive on through the Lone Star State, stopping once at a motel to take showers, but not to sleep. Through Bayard's dickering we get the room at half price. Now as nighttime begins once again, we are on very flat land. The sun goes down in a golden, shimmering halo which nearly blinds us,

92

and then we are swallowed in a very black night on an arrow-straight road. Although I have the gas to the floorboard most of the time, the car doesn't seem to be moving. It's as if we are in Outer Space with no familiar landmarks around by which to judge speed. A slight grayish mist hangs over the macadam highway, like one would expect over the River Styx. Suddenly, no more than twenty-five feet ahead, I see a riderless horse gallop across the road. My foot shoots off the gas. "Goddam! Did you-all see that? A horse, horse. It went right across the road there."

"Where, where?" Bayard says. "I didn't see a thing."

I cut the speed down, slowly pick it back up, and then, as I am wondering what in the world a horse was doing loose on a highway, I witness a brownish colt with white marks on her dart across the road not more than ten feet away. I see her nostrils flare. "Jesus, another one! You saw her, didn't you? That one was as plain as day."

"Let me take the wheel," Bayard says. "You've been driving too long."

He climbs over Abigail for the wheel, and we do not stop for the changeover. The boys in the back are fighting, Joey is crying, and Abigail halfheartedly tries to separate them one minute and the next flies into them in a rage. In front we talk in slow phrases as if drugged. The car, under Bayard's foot pressure, is going over ninety. And then I see light in the distance, a twinkling yellow light, a pinprick on the horizon. "What's that out there? You see that, don't you?"

"That must be El Paso," Bayard says.

"Hot dog! Ten more minutes and we can lie in a bed and get some sleep. Man, oh, man."

We drive on and on. The pinprick of yellow grows into a sparkling, alive form out there. Half an hour passes, then an hour. The lights now seem so close that the town could not possibly be more than a mile or so away. Still we drive, and the lights only broaden on the skyline, but do not open up into a town. You never see this phenomenon in the hills of Tennessee.

By dawn the bunched-up lights have separated and we enter El Paso. We've been two nights without a bed, and I insist on checking in a motel. Bayard wants to deposit Abigail at her ex-in-laws', and then take the bus for Tucson. If we check in a motel, he explains, we'll have to postpone Tucson until the next day. Sleeping is a waste of time. But I can't concentrate; my body takes forever to unravel itself from the car; and words come from others, it seems, from the far end of a tunnel. I must get into a bed and sleep. I'll die if I don't. Abigail wants some rest before facing her ex-in-laws. Bayard loses. We all check into a motel suite with three beds: Bayard, Abigail, the kids, and I. I shut my eyes, see the macadam road still in front of me, and cannot sleep. But soon Bayard and Abigail are profoundly unconscious. Abigail snores with her mouth wide open, and Bayard's head hangs to the side as if his neck was broken. The kids cuddle up into balls. I try several ways to sleep, but cannot. Finally I get up, drink a warm beer, and read a day-old local newspaper. There are items, most to be continued, about hometown murders, rapes, and corruption—very important news to El Paso, totally without interest to Illinois. I know I am traveling, which curiously refreshes me, and I begin looking forward to seeing the sights that night.

Our one night on the town, it turns out, is to cross the border and look in on Juarez. A slim, good-natured young man— one of the ex-in-laws—is our guide, and he takes us to a cabaret with a floor show. (Thinking in terms of Terre Haute, I

94

ask where the whorehouses are. "Just look around you," the ex-in-law says, through a knowing smile, "they're all over the place.") We sit ringside at the cabaret, the ex-in-law, Bayard and Abigail and I. It is a relief not to have the kids with us, and we all start in heavily on the tequila. A nightclub comic with an obvious toupee is telling a few locally oriented jokes in English (most of the clientele is American), and then he introduces a dancer named Janine. "Give her a big hand, ladies and gentlemen, and she'll do her stuff."

A beautiful raven-haired girl floats out from the wings, dressed in a harem costume that leaves her midriff bare. Drenched in a bluish spotlight, she twists and turns, showing off an exemplarily stacked body. "O.K., ladies and gentlemen," the comic is crooning into a mike, "Janine will now allow one gentleman from the audience to dance with her. Don't stampede, fellows. She can only dance with one at a time."

No one is rushing onstage, but there Janine continues to turn and show those pale, well-turned legs. I drain another shot of tequila. I'll show the world what kind of man I am. "Here. I'll dance with the lady."

The spotlight goes on us, and I hold her snugly in my arms. She's about a foot shorter than I am. Here come the three dance steps I learned so well in Tennessee, followed by a "dip," and then I speak in her ear as I used to do at the old country-club affairs: "Jesus, you dance great, baby. Let's meet outside after this show. How about it?"

She nods, smiling a little.

"O.K., O.K.," I say. How do you like that? I'm only in the nightclub five minutes, and already I have a date with the lead dancer. What a lover! I wink, and go back to my table. One spotlight stays on me, and another follows Janine as she goes on with her harem number. Do they have the spotlight on me because I've made out?

"And now, ladies and gentlemen, for the first time this evening little Janine will do her world-famous striptease."

She takes off a ribbon, her diaphanous blouse, and then swirls, with fingers plucking at her bra hooks. She wears a purple, spangled bra. With bra tantalizingly unhooked, she stops and stands bolt upright. From a snaredrum someplace comes an ominous roll, as if the high-wire act is reaching its climax. Then the bra is flung aside with a flourish, and there before us stands someone with breasts as flat as an Indian brave's and nipples the size of a dime. While my brain ricochets through tequila and beer and two sleepless nights, I hear laughter all around and mad clapping. Janine races away, and the spotlight stays on me.

"Boy, if you could have seen your face," Bayard says, doubling up. "I'd give a thousand dollars if I'd had a camera then."

I have no anger or real shame. I've been made to look a fool, but what's so new about that? In fact, all the attention I'm getting isn't so difficult to take. What I can't get over is that my eyes, ears, reasoning, and touch told me something that wasn't so. My desires—and clutching at straws to make them come true—had led me into this blunder: making a pitch at a transvestite. (Years later I stumbled into a museum in Rome, and spied the nude backside of a voluptuous, reclining woman. Ambling around to the front, I discover that the sculptor has fiendishly placed male genitals on the statue. The male guards at this museum seemed to enjoy the look of surprise on the tourists' faces. It broke the boredom.) When you want something, how you can be made to pay! Girls who go to Hollywood, middle-aged women who take correspondence courses to become writers. Carnival workers and popular evangelists know the American heart as well as anyone. I wanted to write a book and lord it over folks at home, and here I am in Mexico on my way to Tucson to pick up a motorcycle for someone like an old-time darkie. But I believed— I *had* to believe—that whatever Lowney and Jones told me was true. Lowney told me there was a great book in me.

But who was I? Lurching from the men's room, I pass a series of dimly lit tables which are occupied by single women. Strong perfume reaches out, and here and there a smile. A coffee-colored woman with peroxide hair smiles the most and my eyes hook on to hers. Her breasts strain from out of an uplift bra, the dark cleavage looking a foot long. "May I buy you a drink?" I say.

Her smile doubles, and a bubbly concoction comes to her with the speed of a bullet. I take another double shot of tequila with lemon and salt. Would Juanita be proud of my knowing how to drink tequila? The peroxide woman smiles, watching the comic on stage, one hand around her drink, the fingers of the other stroking my cock.

"Is there a room we can go to?" I say.

"¿*Que?*"

"A room . . . a bed . . . " I point to her, to me, and then pantomime the posture of sleep.

The blonde jabs her thumb upwards. Soon we climb a creaky flight of stairs to the floor above the nightclub. She leads me first into a well-lit room where a plump, middle-aged woman in a nurse's white uniform sits behind a desk. "Hello, let me see it," the nurse-woman says, in a pleasing Spanish accent. I do a short arm in front of her, and she watches closely. Then she writes something in a medical ledger, and follows with a brisk scrubbing of my genitals.

Was this an elaborate con job to allay any fears of catching the clap?

In a small room, almost as well lit as the nurse's quarters, I lie nude on a swaybacked bed and observe the blonde divest herself of a whalebone bra, an expansive corset, and panties five times too tight. Flesh is jumping out all over the place. No, she doesn't understand what a "half 'n half" or an " 'arf 'n 'arf" is. She doesn't understand an embarrassed pantomime either. She smiles tiredly; money has already been exchanged. She doesn't have to sell me anything else. It's service time now. I calmly observe all that is going on, but in a state of paralysis on my back. The tequila has affected me that way. I am lucid, but I can't turn over. She starts to mount me, and the bedsprings fall a yard.

"Wait. Put this on me first." I have taken a condom from my wallet before stretching out.

"No. Bad." She pantomimes the posture of the nurse-woman. "A pro. After. Come on, Joe."

I am in a foreign country. Juarez, Mexico. Clap is waiting to get me, I know. The condom slides on, followed by 350 pounds of blonde womanhood. She goes through an eye-rolling, heavy-breathing simulation of an orgasm, cooing in Spanish, and it triggers the necessary response from me. . . . It is over. She helps me up like a knocked-out fighter and leads me back to the room with the nurse-woman. "Hello," the nurse says, "you want a pro?"

The condom didn't break, but why not double insurance? It's free. A big production is made out of washing my privates in formaldehyde, and then I'm given a tiny tube of white ointment to shoot up my tool. "Leave it in as long as you can before pissin'," my nurse says.

Downstairs, I surprise the blonde by buying her a drink

and sitting awhile longer with her. She doesn't know what to do, beginning to jab her thumb toward upstairs after a while. But I only want to pretend affection—in fact, I do feel affection—touching her hand, acting something out in pantomime, smiling and nodding at her. I put on the look I used to give Juanita after we had made love. Those at the ringside table know what I've been up to, and I'm glad. I return and as they kid me, I keep a knowing, satisfied grin on my face.

Outside the nightclub a small boy pulls at my wrist. "Hey, mister," he whispers in my ear, "my sister. A virgin. You want to fuck her? Only two blocks away."

A shabbily dressed man corrals Bayard. "Hey, you want a show tonight? Two girls. Young. Clean. They suck each other. You watch."

The ex-in-law shoos them away like flies. We pick up several bottles of tequila to take back with us across the border. They are dirt cheap. Driving back toward the lights of El Paso, I fantasize Juanita waiting at the motel.

In the morning Bayard and I take the bus to Tucson, leaving Abigail and her boys waiting behind in El Paso. The countryside has a reddish dust, a scrub or cactus here and there, and for long stretches is uninhabited as far as the eye can see. At every stop, Bayard and I gulp down beer for our hangovers until the driver honks his horn for us to reboard. Here I am, I think, sitting beside a Colony Veteran and almost feeling equal to him. The bus bounces, and Bayard cradles the side of his face with his hand. "Wonder how being married to Abigail would be?" he drawls. "I've sort of thought about it now and then."

"Not bad probably. She knows how to rough it," I say, feeling like a heretic from Lowney's teaching and thinking how much better built Juanita was than Abigail and how much more in control of things.

"Lowney'd blow her stack if she knew about her," he says. "Listen. Whatever you do, don't have a slip of the tongue about us driving down with Abigail in her car. You'll remember, won't you? We came all the way by bus."

"God, Bayard, don't worry about that."

"Sometimes you just want to take a rest from Lowney. You know?"

"Sure. Boy, I know it," I say, enjoying being flippant about Lowney—like having a taste of freedom from a worrisome obsession—but not wanting to go too far. Bayard, I remember, has passed on to Lowney some of the things I have said.

"There's another thing I guess I better let you in on so you won't be too shocked. Can you keep a secret?"

"Yes."

"You swear?"

"I swear."

"Lowney and Jim are . . . you know . . . it's more than just pupil and teacher."

"Yeah?" Somehow I'd always known it without being told. It was something I didn't want to dwell on.

"Now if she should tell you herself, don't you let on that I've already told you. You promise?"

"O.K., I promise."

At the Tucson bus station Sid meets us. Blond hair cut a quarter inch from his scalp, sun crinkles wedged in the sides of his eyes, wearing sloppy moccasins, a touch of B.O. He informs Bayard of Lowney's and Jim's current mood and explains what life is like in Tucson. He is in the exalted position of being part of this year's Winter Traveling Team. He has seen many seasons with the Colony, and deigns to barely ac-

100

knowledge me, a latecomer to it all. His book ("which is gonna knock 'em on their asses") is nearly finished—or so Lowney has said over and over.

"Oh, yeah, I guess I better tell you something else," Sid says over a beer, before we go out. "Montgomery Clift is staying here for a few days."

Montgomery Clift!

"He's trying to get the lowdown from Jim on how he should play Prewitt in the movie. He doesn't get in the way too much, and he's probably not a bad guy."

A movie star! Someone larger than life, whose face has appeared on that screen that has all but conquered the minds of our generation. Someone in the sea of all those beautiful Hollywood women. Someone who is known the moment he takes a step on the street. He has Fame. But an inner voice tells me not to get too giddy over his presence: Be cool, don't show your emotions to a celebrity.

The stucco house is on a quiet, very middle-class street. A water sprinkler flicks around, putting a cool, refreshing splatter on the deep green grass. Jim's trailer is parked on a court a mile away, and he seldom uses it now. Lowney gives us her happy greeting, washed over by her white, extraordinary smile. "The mind may lie fallow this winter, but we're going to turn out some terrific books from this Colony yet. I can't wait to knock those New York hicks on their asses. Are you working regularly back in Marshall, Johnny?"

"I've got over two hundred pages."

"Copy. I can't tell you how helpful copying is. Copy. Copy"—the concerned frown showing. "And I heard you went home for Christmas," the white smile reblossoming.

"Aw, I was there a couple of days."

"Did you see that girl friend?"

101

"I bumped into her, yeah."

"You've got a hell of a book in you"—the frown coming back—"but you've got to forget the things of this world if you're going to pull it out. You've got to forget Success and lose that Ego. Copy. A woman is probably going to get you, though. Your mind is too full of cunt. I predict this: Two years hence you will be married. Listen, everybody." Jim and Bayard were in the spotlessly clean kitchen with us. "Two years from now Johnny will be married. Not to just any girl, but to a rich one. See if I'm not right. I'd bet a million on it."

"If they cut open his brain," Jim twangs, "I bet a lot of little cunts would spring out. Just like when they cut open Tom Wolfe's brain all those TB germs popped out."

"How's that old woman in the house treating you?" Lowney says. "Is she making life impossible? I know that woman."

"No. Actually, we get along fine. But there is something I guess I should tell you." The need to let someone know, but feeling mean and low at being a tattletale. Lowney had advice on everything else; she must have ideas on this. "Jud has a real violent side none of you have seen. The other day he exploded in the kitchen while we were washing the dishes— telling me how he was going to smash me and my car and so forth. All I ever did to him was ask that he contribute toward gas money if he could. He's going to go crazy one of these days, I tell you."

"It's that old woman, I'm sure," Lowney says. "Stirring trouble up between you."

"No, it's not that. He's peculiar, I mean really peculiar. You know how he always clears his throat and then speaks slowly in a very low key. Well, it was like another person: a booming voice and his arm muscles swelling up." They were all smiling; they didn't realize the scope of this thing. "And he has this yen for old women."

Lowney tosses back a lock of gray-streaked hair, the smile frozen on her face; Jones stares at me.

"I mean—you know—*really* old women. Women who are all gray-headed. He talks about making them."

"Look, if you get tough right back at him," Jim says, "I bet he will leave you alone. I know this kind of guy. They don't listen until they think you might knock the shit out of 'em."

"Bayard," Lowney says, "are you copying at home like I told you to . . . ?"

It is evening now. Bayard and I have been out exploring the terrain around Tucson, and we come in the front door. A man sits in the corner by lamplight. He wears gray flannel trousers, loafers, and a shirt without tie. His black hair sticks up in front, and his features are as strong as a hawk's. His greenish eyes come right at you with an unmistakable intensity. "Monty, here are two of my boys who just arrived today. You haven't met them yet."

We shake hands, and he returns to the conversation he has been having with Lowney and Jim. " . . . Lancaster has billing over me, so I'm not going to let him grab the picture as well . . . " His voice is higher-pitched and more jumpy than I had expected.

"Monty . . . Monty," Lowney is going, "listen to me. It'd help you a hell of a lot in this role if you had more background in Americana. And it's all around you for the taking. Read."

"What should I read? What books?"

"Have you read *U. S. A.* yet? Dos Passos?"

"No, what's that?"

103

"He's one of the greatest writers in this country, and he has the feel of the country in that book. Jesus Christ, what a writer before he got religion and turned into Henry Luce! Read *U. S. A.* Copy some of it. What those stumblebums and drifters are thinking about and doing. You can learn a hell of a lot there. Try Steinbeck. *The Grapes of Wrath,* but don't believe all you read there. *The Ears of Johnny Bear* you should study. It's about a gigantic, moronic monster who can mimic and recite everything he overhears. . . . "

"Hey, that's Lancaster. The Monster." Clift stands and gives an ape imitation, his laugh afterwards a quick, falsetto titter that I don't remember him using on screen. I notice that he is drinking a lot. As he sits back down, one long leg goes over the arm of the chair.

"And if you want to know how Prewitt talks, listen to this boy here," Lowney beats on, pointing to me. "He talks like somebody from Harlan, Kentucky. That's where my people come from too. I've told Jim all he knows about that region. That stuff in *Eternity* about Uncle John Turner comes straight from my own uncle."

Jim, in a tight T-shirt, draws his breath in, his deep chest going out to its limits, and then lets out the air slowly. He doesn't comment.

"Listen to this boy talk. He may be a relative of mine for all we both know. He's Prewitt. Listen to him."

But I don't get a chance to open my mouth, she's talking so much.

A few days pass. Lowney and Jim spend their time with Montgomery Clift, taking pictures of him, driving him around, going to restaurants. Bayard, Sid, and I haunt beer joints and explore the countryside; after the briefest of instructions, I am blasting down streets on a motorcycle. Then

Clift catches a plane for Hollywood, and anecdotes and fine points of his personality are gone over by us as if we were all autograph hounds outside Schwab's drugstore. Lowney tells how "Monty" has driven the same Buick for many years and how tight he is with money. Sidney thinks he noticed a bald spot beginning on the back of Monty's head. Jim relates how Clift and Elizabeth Taylor worked together—imagine that—in *A Place in the Sun.* "He says that she can instantly catch a mood. Nothing has to be explained. He'd rather work with her than any other actress in the world. It's all intuition with her."

Anecdotes pile up: the time in the restaurant when there was no silverware and Monty ate his salad with his fingers ("He calls salad 'garbage.'"); the late evening when Monty fell out of the car while Lowney was driving and rolled all the way down a clay hill ("I thought to shit he was dead for sure. But when I got down to him on the bottom, he was giggling. He may drink too much, Jim." "Shit, he'd-a been dead if he hadn't-a been drunk then."); the occasion when he made a play for a teen-age girl, proving—according to Lowney—that he had interests in girls.

I am leaning around a doorjamb, looking into a softly lit bedroom and saying good night. It is a very contented, happy tableau. Two people lie stretched out on the bed, the sheet, for decorum's sake, pulled up to their chins. The whites of the woman's eyes stand out against the deep tan of her face, and her smile shows those milk-white teeth that are still standing up perfectly well into middle age. The man squirms about in embarrassed maleness. He seems shy and vulnerable in this moment.

In the afternoon we all go to a movie in downtown Tucson. While the newsreel sputters to scenes around the world,

Lowney elbows me and points excitedly to a couple talking in front of us. I listen, and hear Spanish being spoken. "They're speaking a foreign language," Lowney whispers fiercely. "Imagine!" The movie is *Moulin Rouge,* and afterwards, back at the shaded, stucco house, Lowney says, "Of all the pretentious shit I've seen in my life, that takes the cake. That artsy-fartsy color. And that romanticizing of a drunk made me want to puke."

"Some people . . . some"—Jim is weighing his words—"some people, Lowney, just have to drink. You don't understand."

"I understand drunks, and there's nothing romantic about them. Haven't I been married to one for twenty-five years? Don't tell me I don't know drunks. Every male drunk—I don't care who he is—is showing off. He may cry that he's a tragic figure, but he's nothing but a show-off."

In the morning we tour the mountains, courtesy of our host and hostess, stopping at a copy of an Old World Inn for lunch. Shafts of sunlight filter through high windows, the wooden planked floor gleams, and the waitresses pad around in what looks like Swiss peasant garb. The menu shows astronomical prices, but our host and hostess are in a holiday mood. No boiled potatoes and hot Jell-o today. After much coaxing, Lowney orders her one kind of drink: a sidecar. She orders it, but she takes only a few sips. During the meal Jim orders champagne, and its bubbles fizz in our glasses up into the clean, clear sunshine. This is what you can afford to do if you write a best seller.

In town Jim wants to see *Limelight* with Charlie Chaplin, and it turns out that I am the only one who agrees to go with him. Lowney has a headache; Bayard and Sid have work to do on the motorcycles. Jim seems a little embarrassed that only I spoke up, and I feel uncomfortable, yet proud, in being alone with the author of *From Here to Eternity* on an afternoon expedition. As we approach the box office, Jim fumbles with his billfold, looking left and right. Does he expect me to pay my own way? I'm supposed to be indigent, like all Colony underlings. Doesn't he know that? He hesitates, then mumbles for two tickets. He further purchases two cartons of hot buttered popcorn, and with our knees up on the seat in front we watch Charlie Chaplin and the beautiful, young Claire Bloom. The melodrama, of course, is about an old music-hall comic who saves a young dancer from suicide, nourishes her back to health, and helps her rise to stardom on the stage. Then he himself becomes unwanted as an artist and dies a tear-jerking death while performing in a comic-relief role the girl wangles for him in one of her starring vehicles.

Driving back in the green Chrysler, Jim sits reflectively, not driving at his usual racetrack speed. "You know," he says softly, in a tone I'd never heard him use before, "most people never know what misery other people are going through. There is just no way to let people understand in this society."

*

A new face was blushing in the house when we returned. This was Arnold, a student at the University of Arizona, who had come originally with vigor and high confidence some weeks back to interview Jim for the student newspaper and had stayed to be worked by degrees into Colony status. He wore this night a bright yellow sport shirt that someone had starched and carefully ironed. The rest of us were in Levi's and T-shirts, Lowney in her usual sweat shirt, sans bra, with the sleeves pushed up.

We sat in a circle on the floor. Arnold peered through shiny horn-rims, and his black curly hair shot up from his scalp past Colony limits. He had a way of speaking, and then ducking his head as if expecting a blow. His voice was deep, tentative. "Wallace Stevens I've always thought was our best poet," Arnold is saying, then ducking. "Are you familiar with him, Lowney?"

"Wallace Stevens. I know him. He's the biggest horse's ass in the country. Look at that one"—and she points to Sidney, leaning back on elbows. "When he came in with us, he was spouting T. S. Eliot. I once caught him and Jim mouthing that crap at each other in Jim's trailer. If I hadn't clipped it in the bud they'd be la-de-da-ing at one another right this minute. *Forget literature!* But I don't think you've got what it takes anyhow. Tell me. If I gave you three wishes, what would you wish for? Tell me."

"I—I——"—face scarlet. All of us, except for Lowney and Arnold, are back on our elbows. "I'd like to write a book as good as . . . *The Naked and the Dead.* Also, *Eternity.*"

"You got a girl friend, ain't you?" Jim says. We're all getting cracks at Arnold. There's a delirious strangeness in being considered now a Colony Vet. The sadistic pleasure of a fraternity man looking over a new pledge.

"Yes—I—uh—have a girl friend. She was the one with me when I first came to interview you."

"A mousy little thing," Lowney says. "Not a peep out of her. But I could tell she was looking down her nose at us. What does she do?"

"She's on the school paper. We work together."

Image now of Arnold strolling on campus with a quiet, pretty girl, her fingers stained with ink. There were no oaks

108

that I knew of in Tucson, but I saw Arnold and this black-haired girl beneath the lush green foliage of that tree.

"Are you fucking her?" Jim wants to know. Here we go.

Arnold looks all around, stunned. "Yeah."

"Well, you're never going to write," Lowney says. "You think you're hot shit because some dumb little dame has been making eyes over you. What you want to do is spout this intellectual crap and have people go ooh-la-la. I'm not going to have you coming into my Colony and fucking things up. *You* want to write. Look at this boy"—pointing to me, causing my chest to rise—"he's writing a hell of a book. He's telling painful things. He's holding nothing back and he's giving up everything. Listen, you'll never be an artist until you hit bottom."

The bottom. At the Colony I used to go around wondering if I'd hit the bottom yet. Lowney said so many times that one couldn't be an artist until the bottom was reached that I tried to force myself down. *"Lose that ego,"* she screamed, and I sank myself further into a trance of debasement. I wasn't altogether sure, though, what *ego* meant to her. As she spoke of it (in nearly every conversation), I pictured a shiny white ball that one could grab from within one's self and fling away. Without ego, one took punishment; one didn't fight back; one took others' opinions as gospel. Your own ideas were worthless. You were defeated. If she said that was what it took to write, then it must be so. You couldn't win until you had lost.

"I do want to write," Arnold says.

"Then quit that fucking college. If you're ready to write by next spring, then I'll take you back with us to the Colony. But I doubt most sincerely if you've got the guts to give up

109

worldly things. You'll probably knock up that mousy little girl is what you'll do. *They all want to fill their wombs!"*

The Colony Vets go to the refrigerator for cans of beer, a decided and daring privilege. Arnold sits, cross-legged, no beer offered, his socks drooping and looking somehow pathetic against his white skin. Intellectual socks, a non-member-of-the-Colony's socks. I was so proud to be a Vet. But I couldn't articulate to myself the beginnings of another terrible feeling: Don't let them take charge of you. They have no right. It's your life, your privacy. Stay with the girl!

In the morning Bayard and I prepare for the motorcycle ride back, the *raison d'être* of our trip. After a few last-minute instructions, a couple of warm-up swings around the block, I am given charge of the oldest Harley-Davidson in the Tucson stable, a red brute with an old-fashioned hand gearshift by the gas tank. Goods stuffed in saddlebags, a pair of wavy discolored goggles over my eyes, I brace myself aboard its bucking frame and look to Bayard to lead us off toward the horizon. He sits easily on Jim's tan, chromium-sparkling machine, gunning the motor lazily. His has an automatic starter and a fancy gearshift, operated by a flick of the toe. "I'll watch out for him, Lowney," Bayard calls, jerking his thumb toward me. "I'll see we get back safe. Don't worry."

"If something happens, I'll never forgive you, Bayard. Now"—to me—"copy when you get back. Let scenes just flow from your mind. Don't think about how many pages you have. . . . We'll see you in the spring!"

The road to El Paso and Abigail was straight and slightly tilted down. Bayard took bursts of speed in front of me, going out like a Yo-Yo and then drawing back, his spine straight, elbows out from his side. I watched my speedometer climb to eighty-five, and still I didn't have the throttle all the way open. What a sensation! The wind tore at my head and the scenery, through my discolored, blinderlike goggles, became streaks. How vulnerable you were on this machine. My feet were only inches away from the flying macadam. Bayard glided around everything in our path—pickup trucks, passenger cars, diesel rigs—in an easy, fluid motion. I followed, thrilling at the way my machine shot forward with just a squeeze of the throttle. How beautiful to be so vulnerable, yet powerful enough to leave everything in your path standing still. And there Bayard roared around a long, high trailer truck as if he were a bee. In the deliciousness of being in total command of my machine I was forgetting the scare stories about potholes that could flip you over or the mysterious high-speed "wobble" that could send you sailing in the air. (Jim particularly loved to dwell on the high-speed wobble, telling how he'd nearly killed himself in the grip of one.) But I was in command now; nothing could happen I didn't will. The speedometer showed nintey-three. The trailer truck in front was now emitting a wealth of evil black smoke that went directly into my lungs. Ninety-three did not seem any faster than fifty. It was a straightaway, and *Bayard* had passed. I turned the throttle on full, felt the beast respond as if kicked, and I swung into the left lane. Halfway around the smoke-belching monster I saw the other trailer truck. It was coming at me like a locomotive, taking up all the left lane. "A mistake," I wanted to say. "I'll go back. Wait a minute." But I didn't have a chance. I had to take aim at the dividing line, all the room I had, and draw my shoulders and knees in like a foetus. As the black glob came abreast, I looked up at the driver's face—pale and needing a shave, mouth open. His eyes caught mine in an etched moment and then he was

111

gone. He had to throw his right wheels off the road and onto gravel to avoid killing me. When I finally got clear of the trailer trucks, I motioned to Bayard for a rest stop. He pulled into the one filling station in a drowsy little hamlet—giving a crisp arm signal—and we dismounted.

"God damn, I pulled a beaut back there," I said, trying for casualness. "Did you see it?"

"Yeah, but I've shaved them closer than that. It's a hell of a lot of fun, I know, but I wouldn't do it again until you get more experience."

The old-timers lounging around the station—some in chairs kicked back against the stucco building, eyes crinkling under Stetsons—observed us with faint smiles. We got gas, drank Cokes and belched, and strutted about. Then Bayard started his tan Harley, gunned it, and waited for me to rev up. I kicked down on the red machine, down and down and down. Not even a sputter. The old-timers turned their eyes away, and their smiles grew. Bayard left his own machine and ambled over with his crooked smile. "Get off. I'll try her." He lazily threw a leg over, fiddled with his foot on the kick starter a moment, then jumped up and came down viciously. It started, and roared. Pulling on my goggles, I felt a slight sting on my cheeks.

That night in El Paso we told Abigail and her ex-in-laws all about Montgomery Clift, every detail, and got drunk. But no one seemed to be nearly as interested in him as we were. Only people trying for fame themselves can be bowled over by the famous. Abigail cut into my description of Clift's bald spot sharply: "Go look at your face in the mirror. My God, it's making me sick."

Looking at it, I jumped myself. Around the eyes where the goggles had fit the flesh was milk white; the rest, a flaming red. I smeared a handful of vaseline over my cheeks, and the next day I put on a leather helmet and fixed a scarf to flutter over my mouth like a World War I ace. Now only a scant line of flesh was bare to wind and sun. Bayard, brown as a nut, had no trouble. He led our three-vehicle caravan, Abigail following in her battered Ford convertible, and me taking up the rear and the fumes from Abigail's exhaust. On boring long stretches Bayard would perform trick riding—standing on the seat with one foot, sticking the other out behind, and leaning over to steer. He sat on the seat backwards and drove with his elbows on the handlebars, smiling his crooked smile back at us. He dipped from side to side, having to throw his foot down occasionally for support. "Bayard, I wish you'd stop that kind of riding," Abigail said at a rest stop, cigarette sparks flying. "You're making me so nervous I can't drive."

In Oklahoma, funds growing slim, we decide to eat some provisions we'd brought along from El Paso in a picnic area by the side of the road. Then we discover a problem. No water. Fortunately, we have a water can and we sight a motel across the highway—white with brown trim and tile roof, prosperous-looking.

Water bucket in hand, Bayard and I confidently stroll up the gravel path to a door marked, "Office." A man steps out, frowning, before we get there. I am a recent college grad, white, Baptist (*manque*), someone accustomed to getting along splendidly with shopkeepers. (The only time I had ever been treated as a second-class citizen was when I had been wearing the uniform of my country.) "Pardon us, sir," I say, muting my twang, "but could you please spare us a little water?"

"We don't have any." His eyes go up Bayard and down

me, lingering a moment on my Lindbergh helmet and goggles. We are motorcycle riders—worse still, possibly *Okies*. No one hates Okies, we find out, like an Oklahoman.

"Could you tell us where we might find some? We're parked across the road in the picnic area."

"Try twenty-five miles up the road."

"But we got some young kids with us," Bayard says, trying for heartbreak. "They're crying for water. We can't make twenty-five miles."

"I told you we don't have any water. Try someplace else."

We try the next motel up the highway and the next and the next. The same answer: No water; go somewhere else. We find a supply of tepid water at last in a dust-coated filling station, and can have all we want, the attendant, whose clothes are grimier than ours, tells us. But by this time we are too far from the picnic area for it to do us any good. We go to a roadside café, two motorcycle riders, a nervous woman, and two fighting children—a strange tableau anywhere—and are given a back table. The waitress does not smile at our jokes, and the egg sandwiches we eat lay like lead in our stomachs for hours afterwards. By nightfall, still in the land of the Okie, we keep having trouble with motels. A cheerful, welcoming "Vacancy" sign glows, but when Bayard and I clomp into the office, the registry book closes and it's all filled for the night. By the third turndown we get the picture. "All right, Abigail," Bayard drawls. "You got to get the room—say it's for you and the kids. We'll have to slip in."

Bayard and I park our machines in some bushes and watch Abigail go into the Colonial-style motel, a child in each hand, a Pall Mall in her mouth. A woman comes out with her and leads her to an outside room. It's the second from the end. After the woman goes back to the office, we wait five minutes and then we blast to the room and bolt the door behind us. Breath recovered, relief at last, we open one of our prized bottles of Juarez tequila, ninety-eight cents the quart. I lick salt off the back of my hand, take a suck at a lemon, and then swig the hot yellowish liquid. I've come a long way from Tennessee. If I could only tell Juanita about meeting Montgomery Clift. . . . And then I'm dancing around the room with Abigail, music from a quarter-fed radio. A few more shots of tequila, and the usual happens. I fall over on top of her, pressing her down on the bed. The desire for connection will not be stilled. Friendly girl, she begins throwing her pelvis back, in a sort of primitive code. Dot dash, dot dot dash. Her pelvic bone is strong and pointed and lifts me up and down like a fork. Bayard'll understand, I tell myself; he's a Colony man. But someone's prying us loose, turning me over by the shoulders. "Come on," Bayard says, "come on now." I pretend drunkenness, something not hard to do. Bayard and Abigail take one bed, the kids the other, and I occupy the floor.

By Missouri my face can no longer take it, despite helmet, goggles, scarf, and layers of vaseline. A thin streak on my forehead and two tender patches below my eyes turn raw and ooze a clear evil fluid. I cannot smile, and have to talk with my mouth puckered in a permanent O, as if waiting to be kissed. It rains as we go through one town, and I fight to keep my motorcycle from skidding away beneath me on streetcar tracks. Pellets of rain wiggle down my goggles, and my engine dies at a traffic light—while I watch Bayard and his needed pile-driving leg rounding a corner up ahead. As horns sound behind me, I leap up, pray, and come down solid on the kick-pedal. Miraculously it starts and I catch up with the caravan, waving them to the side of the road.

"I don't care anymore," I say, my little ball of ego gone. "I can't go on. I give up."

"Aw, you're doing fine," Bayard drawls. "It won't be long before we're home. This is fun."

"No, this is crazy, particularly with this rough weather. It's got to end." My words, coming from the pit of my stomach, impress him—and me. We find a mechanic who attaches the red motorcycle to a trailer hitch on the back of Abigail's car, removing the motorcycle's front wheel to do it and placing it in the trunk. Now I sit again behind the wheel of Abigail's car, dragging cigarettes and swilling warm beer. My bike follows without me aboard. Bayard, I note from time to time, keeps to a steady pace in front, no trick stunts, his shoulders seeming to draw in more and more. Farther into Missouri it snows, light drifts that whirl down. When we stop for rests—about every hour now—Bayard's teeth chatter and his eyes look wild. He tries for a manly, Jones-esque description of how it is to drive in snow, but the bravado is thin. After an hour or two in the car, my mouth loses its pucker and the raw wounds close.

Driving along, I impulsively tell Abigail about Juanita, bringing in Lowney's comments on women, which have now become my own. "They all want to fill wombs, make a nest," I parrot.

"I don't believe that's altogether true," Abigail says, reaching around to slap one of her whining boys. "But I'll say one thing for that woman, though. She sure has a hold over you guys. It's almost unbelievable. I couldn't last two seconds in that Colony and I don't think any other woman could either."

"But we're artists. Serious writers."

"You're still young and human and alive." Abigail is quiet

116

a moment, as if considering whether to go on with this line of thought or not. "Did you know I was in the Army?" she says at last.

"No. Where? I was in Korea."

"I was stateside, in an Army hospital. And I never will forget this one young soldier who died. He was eighteen. He came in complaining of just a simple stomachache, and before the medics could get around to diagnosing it, he died of a ruptured appendix. Bang. Just like that. They laid him out all by himself in this room—an examining room—and I couldn't keep away from him for some reason. He was nude and so perfect and it didn't seem possible he was dead. I couldn't help myself. His feet were unmarked, no corns or calluses or things you find on older people. He was finely muscled all over, no fat or anything. He had an uncircumcised penis—I can see it now—and his testicles lay there like two perfect little eggs. I held his penis for a while and moved my hand through his pubic hair. He didn't have any hair on his chest, not one hair that I could find. He had shaved that morning and there was a little nick by his Adam's apple. . . . Oh, I wasn't the only one impressed by him. Some nurses came in, just to gaze. And a few doctors. I don't know why I'm telling you about him or what's the point. It's just that his dying seemed such a waste, terribly unnecessary. It broke your heart, you couldn't believe it. You kept thinking he might get up and walk away any minute. . . . "

*

Back in Illinois, mission accomplished, I postponed returning to Mrs. Handy's Charles Addams-like home for as long as possible. I freeloaded on Bayard, sleeping between clean sheets at his home, meeting his dimple-cheeked sister back home on a visit from college, and guzzling beer at night in honky-tonks and at non-writers' homes. This extension of the holiday was fine, exhilaratingly irresponsible—but it hadn't been sanctioned by Lowney, and it had to end. Streaking out to Tucson had been Colony business, therefore lawful to be absent from the typewriter. Now it was not. I returned one day at dinnertime, and it was as if Jud and Mrs. Handy hadn't moved. She was drinking coffee with her special extra cream, and he had his legs crossed at the table, purple ankles showing, a drift of tobacco flakes running down his T-shirt. He cleared his throat, face flushed, and smiled oddly.

I emphasized how short the stay had been in Tucson, the hardships along the road, how the wind had cut my face. Something told me to go light on Montgomery Clift, and I did so—just an offhand statement that he had been in Tucson. How had things been going in Marshall? Jud ah-hummed, ah-hummed again, and lit his pipe in a bubbling suck. "We're still writing," Mrs. Handy said, and wanted to know when Lowney and Jones were coming back. Her blue eyes, twinkling, told me she was glad I had returned. She didn't look at Jud.

In my room I found my manuscript still intact under a wad of underwear. Seeing the pages, written in the sober morning hours, relieved me of any lingering holiday mood. Also, in a jumble, were Juanita's fat letters in pink envelopes, her succinct message about where she wished my soul would rot. I propped myself on the bed, and read Juanita's letters once again. I sniffed at the more loving ones, hoping for just a smidgen of her perfume and powder—I knew so well how she smelled—and thought I caught a touch of it. She had left a red-lipsticked kiss on some, and I kissed the imprint back.

St. Valentine's Day had passed while I was on the road—the day my rod was being rode in Juarez, I believe—and I had let it slip without a flower or message to Juanita. St. Valentine's Day had a little extra meaning for us. Two weeks before the holiday—a year ago—Juanita and I had made love our first time. Had it only been a year ago? She had said, "That was my Valentine's gift to you, darling. We couldn't wait, could we?" And on that Valentine's Day I had given her flowers and told her I would love her forever. This year I was a writer and I hadn't written her a line, let alone sent flowers. I was trying to kill her in my mind, and it was killing me.

*

The Colony routine began again, up after a rap on the door by Jud, and then a session of copying other writers before jumping into my own story. Perhaps all that copying of Faulkner and Fitzgerald was taking its toll, for an impending feeling of doom settled over me like a shroud. Jud's step, as he passed unspeaking on the street, seemed livelier—as if he had an edge on me now, despite my Tucson traveling and Montgomery Clift meeting. He smiled goofily at the dinner table one night, and said, "How's your soul these days, John?"

The words rolled in my head before coming to a stop. He had been through my papers and had read Juanita's cry. Two years before I had fist-fought five of my fraternity brothers after one of them had poured water on my sleeping carcass as a joke. Justice had been on my side. In New Orleans, on a post-graduation spree, I had started a fight with a truck driver who kept beating his beer mug on a piano and ruining the piano player's rhythm. Charley Hickerson had pulled my

150 pounds away. ("Don't be crazy, Boney." My college nickname—Boney. "That guy'll kill you.") Now, in the Handy house righteous anger flooded me, magnified because I had predicted Jud would snoop. But the anger couldn't cleanse my newfound sense of unworthiness, the horror of approaching doom. I just looked at him.

The day the letter came from my mother with the clipping inside was a false spring day, bright and warm. As I was slicing open the envelope in my room, a shaft of sunlight ran from the edge of the shade (pulled to the bottom because I couldn't bear the thought of anybody watching me write). I saw Juanita's picture—with an unbecoming hairdo I'd never seen before—and I knew. I put the clipping on the bed, raised the shade, and looked outside. Jud was digging up abandoned carrots in the old garden. I returned to the clipping and saw that Juanita had married someone the week before—shortly after St. Valentine's Day—and that the best man was a false friend of mine. So. She looked terribly stern in the picture, pearls around her neck, a school-graduation shot or a passport photo. I tried thinking of her with the new name, saying it out loud. I had never met her new husband. Had he tried any fancy tricks out on her? His schools and credits were listed, making him out to be someone who would be vaguely interesting in a small town. But how, *how*, could she have written me less than a month before that she was going through the tortures of the damned for me, for love—and now *this*? Was this the ultimate device, the one to finally do it? I pictured calling her home—I started to—and asking her father what the hell was going on. I pictured calling her—her voice subdued and victorious now—and telling her that she had won. Get an annulment, I'll be right down. What a victory haul, marching in and taking her away from this false husband. Then on a real honeymoon we'd laugh about her little mistake.

Yet brimming up, a boiling pot shaking its lid, was the thought that I now had what I needed if I were a true Colony writer: freedom from outside forces. I couldn't be a householder now. I was free. At night I went to every change in features at the local movie house, the few hours during the week it was open. Around ten or fifteen people would be in the audience, Jud on one side of the orchestra, me on the other. (When *Charley's Aunt* with Ray Bolger came for its brief moment, I could see Jud convulsed in the dim streaky light. Everytime Bolger scampered in a long silk dress and bonnet, pursued hotly by a red-faced man in a mistaken-identity crisis, Jud would rock back and forth, snickering out of control. Then afterwards, on the street, going his separate way, he held his bemused, satisfied look, not speaking.) Our household had a standing invitation to watch TV in the house across the street. An energetically social woman said, "Come on over and watch it anytime. We're always there. You'll love *Mr. Peepers.*"

Fight nights the three of us ambled over, only a minute before the opening gong so the amenities were kept to a minimum. The man of the house—out of it completely as so many men in the Midwest were—sat in his easy chair, cane in front, mumbling unheeded directions to his wife about which knob to turn where. "Loud enough for you?" she would bellow. Everyone would nod, except the man of the house who said, "Just a little more!" Mrs. Handy squirming her dress in place under her 85 pounds, crossing her matchstick legs. Before us Carmen Basilio or Jake LaMotta or Sugar Ray or Kid Gavilan or Bobo Olson or—a footnote in history—Gentleman Chuck Davey would be shedding robes, grabbing ropes, chewing

121

mouthpieces, doing dips. "You watch that Chuck Davey," the husband croaked over his cane. "He's as fast as lightning."

Bong! Round one flashed on the screen.

When I was growing up in Tennessee, we did not own a radio for the longest of times. My father's inviolate household principle, during the Depression, was not to buy anything—car, vacation, radio—that offered the slightest chance of pleasure. Books were for wisdom, food was for growth—those commodities we had. The radio only emitted sound, something we could do without. Up the street, some twins, the Bellamy brothers, owned a radio, which I ran to whenever I visited their house. When they were preparing for a family vacation once, I begged them to rent me the radio for fifteen cents. They saw my urgency and settled on a quarter.

I set the radio—about the size of a shoe box—on a card table in the center of our living room and stretched the cord to an overhead outlet. The tuning dial shone majestically orange with black numerals and marks, and it seemed a miracle that tinny sounds came from afar when the center thread aligned itself at certain marks. At dawn—around five A.M.—the stations came in a jumble, like a trick Japanese plant exploding its branches in water, and then in the hot hours of the day boiling itself down to one Knoxville station. At night the far-off signals rushed mysteriously back. I kept the set on all the time except for late-night sleeping, huddled over it, taking meals there, holding the antenna wire to get better reception. I heard guitar and fiddle music, choleric gospel preachers, county agents on heifer and alfalfa problems, dry-voiced women with homemaking hints, and swing music from Cincinnati. The day the Bellamy twins returned, I had to unplug the radio from the ceiling, wrap it in its cord, and lug it back—expecting them to find damage from the intense use. Instead, they put it aside, not even trying it out, and got into a fistfight over something that had happened on their vacation—chasing each other like headless chickens round and round their two-story frame home. Back in my own home I put away the card table, and the cleared space in the living room looked very lonely. Again, we were cut off from outside wavelengths.

On rare special occasions and always by invitation our family trudged across the street to visit the home of rich neighbors who owned a radio with a giant circular dial. The night of the second Louis-Schmeling fight we arrived at the last minute, getting aligned on comfortable seats in a semicircle around the beautiful set. The grown-ups were talking pleasantly when I heard a *gong* and an announcer's raspy, dramatic voice. Faces turned toward the glowing dial, the room became silent, and I sank in wonder. I was in a dark, smoky, electric arena and two men were coming at each other. . . . And then they're saying, "It's over." *Over?* We had just crossed the street! I held my mother's hand, and back across the street we went—not to return again until war should be declared. Now, years later, I was still crossing the street for wavelengths, this time with pictures. Kid Gavilan, a glistening black object, was moving in on Chuck Davey—head ducked, shuffling a little. The white boy, pale and light-haired, was backpedaling and jabbing.

"Watch the Kid give him that bolo punch," the lady of the house said. "I can tell it's coming."

"I ain't never seen anything like it—he just rares back and——" And in the middle of the man of the house's explanantion, Kid Gavilan executed it—a windup pitch that went around in a complete circle before coming home. He caught

Gentleman Chuck on the glottis, knocking the fight right out of him—an undignified way to go.

Our evening pleasure ended, we quietly picked our way back to homebase—the memory of the terror in the white boy's eye, the disbelief after receiving the jolt to the Adam's apple, still registering in my mind.

In the mornings my novel went on, its bulky pages the only proof that I was a writer. "Remember the senses," Lowney had told us over and over. And before jumping into a scene I described the sounds going on and how everything smelled—a way of warming up, like copying. "Be subtle," she cautioned; "leave things out." I held myself tightly over the keyboard. "Make me laugh, make me cry," she had said. "Entertain me!" I tried to be funny on paper, the only place I felt like it. For I knew as I pecked on a typewriter that I had abandoned and betrayed and denied the one I loved. Wasn't I going to be punished?

*

It was after an evening meal of poached eggs on toast, my turn to cook. Mrs. Handy had wiped the crumbs from her lips and had shuffled to other reaches of the house. Jud and I did the dishes. An unshaded, glazed light bulb hung from the low ceiling, throwing shadows against the walls, but bathing the center of the room in stark light. Jud washed, sleeves rolled to mid-biceps. He slowly rubbed a plate or cup in a circle, rinsed it under cold water as if hypnotized, and then handed it to me. I could see holes at the little toes in his canvas shoes. His cheeks had been shaven and were grayishly shiny. I tried to talk, and the words sounded unnatural in my ears, the way words do when you try to cheer up someone who is bedridden while you're still on your feet. A week or two before, he had cleared his throat, sitting with legs crossed at the dinner table, and said, "John, let's go put the gloves on."

"Why? Good Lord, Jud, what earthly good would that do?"

He had smiled inwardly, that bemused, knowing grin, and lit his pipe that was continually going out.

The plates and saucers and forks came so slowly now that I had long spaces with nothing to wipe. The silence was gnawing. Any talk was better than this. "Do you like any of the movies coming out now?" I said. I felt stiff being nice to him, trying to carry on a conversation. At a loss.

"Noooo. I, ah-hum"—carefully, steadily, endlessly washing a plate, one I remembered Mrs. Handy using this night— "haven't seen any good movies lately."

I finally got the plate and turned my back to him, wiping it under the unshaded bulb. "Movies are so corny these days—"

It felt as if something had fallen from the ceiling. I turned, looked up, and felt the next blow catch me squarely on the cheekbone. The plate flew up and I sailed backwards, coming to rest on the floor with my head against the radiator. Jud was over me, fists coming down like pistons. All I could think to do was put my hands over my face and say, "Don't. Please, Jud, don't." Still being nice. As I tried to rise, a fist would catch me and my head would ricochet off iron in a dull thud. Strangely, the blows didn't hurt.

"You're vicious," he screamed—no ah-humms at all. "You're vicious. Vicious!"

I saw he wasn't wearing his glasses. He had taken them off, probably a second before the attack. He was methodical, had perhaps planned this all out beforehand. I noticed idly how hairy his forearms were. His face looked odd, his eyes squinting without his glasses. Then suddenly it stopped. No "Had enough?" or "Taught you a lesson, fellow?" It just stopped, and he turned away.

I felt to see if my nose was broken, and then I ran my tongue around my teeth. One tooth was slightly chipped, leaving a deposit like hard sand on my tongue. Bumps were springing up from my head, and both eyes were closing to slits. I got up to one knee, then to a crouch, finally upright.

There was Mrs. Handy leaning back against the doorjamb, hand to her heart, moaning. "I'm dying. My heart, my heart." I remembered then hearing words from her in the background as Jud was playing my head on the radiator like a xylophone: "Oh, stop it, stop it! Don't kill him, don't kill him!"

"There, there, Mrs. Handy!" I took her by the elbow to lead her away, and looked over my shoulder. Jud was back at the sink, his glasses on, even an apron around his middle. The crazy son of a bitch had begun washing dishes again.

In the Victorian living room I deposited Mrs. Handy to flutter. In the bathroom I threw handfuls of cold water on my face and tried to think. From the kitchen I could hear a delicate shuffling, a rattle of plates, the splatter of water. Wonder if he was down to washing the long bread knife? He could just as easily—and perhaps with a little more sense—have sunk the knife in my back and done the job once and for all. I looked at my reflection in the mirror. It was as if a gang of hornets had been at my face, hardly a space without a lump. Anger bubbled up in me overlapped by a sense of menace and futility. Jud had escalated his madness to its limits. If I fought him now, the complications would be unbearable: the house in shambles, Mrs. Handy dead or being given mouth-to-mouth by a fireman, the winner locked up in the penitentiary, the loser dead. What galled me most, though, was that Jud had so easily got rid of his anger, and now I had to clean up the mess. The only bright spot was that he did not know what I would do. It was now his turn to be apprehensive—if he had any sense left.

"Mrs. Handy," I told her, "I'm going to take you down to your son's house in Robinson. Now don't you worry. Everything is going to be all right. We'll straighten this out."

I weaved into my room for my manuscript and, with it under my arm, led Mrs. Handy to my car in the garage. I turned the ignition and it started, no wires torn out. As we backed into the street, I saw that the kitchen light still burned.

In Robinson, Harry Handy took one look at me and said what I needed was a good drink of whisky. He left the pouring to me, and I sloshed a tumbler half full and drank it down straight. It hardly burned at all. He poured himself a stiff one—or rather more on top of the one he had going—and pushed a Lucky into his black cigarette holder. He was wearing a white T-shirt, sprouts of gray curling over the top, and he had the look of someone who had been expecting a quiet evening alone.

The house was richly furnished with book-lined walls, a curved, gilt-edged mirror over the mantel, and an intricate phonograph system. We weren't even allowed radios at the Colony. How then could there be such a consummate phonograph down here where it all started? Jones had written a huge chunk of *Eternity* in this house, I was told. Locales were pointed out—that desk by the window there, that room overhead—where he had composed certain sections. It was my first time in the house and that was what impressed me most—the areas where Jim had worked on his book. The record collection was Jim's and I noted that there was a lot of jazz and Dixieland. Seeing some symphonies mixed in surprised me for some reason.

"Look, let's get old Bayard over here to see what he thinks," Harry said. "And let's have another drink."

"Thanks, I believe I will."

Bayard burst in a welter of smiles, obviously happy over the new excitement. We were back together again on Colony business, and the painful task of writing could be put aside once more. "Holy Jesus, he really smacked you!" he said, with a beautiful grin. "How did it start?"

"Like I told Lowney and Jim. He's crazy, psychotic. No one believed me and now look what happened. It's a wonder he didn't kill me and Mrs. Handy both."

"He was over him," Mrs. Handy was croaking from the sofa, "hitting him on the head. I kept telling him to stop, but he wouldn't. I never saw anything like it."

"Are you O.K. now, Mom?" Harry said. It seemed a little strange to hear him call her "Mom."

"I'm doing fine."

"Well, what we got to do now," Harry said, pouring himself a final wee one, "is get that bozo out of the house."

Harry drove, Bayard and I next to him in the front seat. We sped over a moon-glistened brick road, farmhouses and silos dark to the left and right. Harry held the steering wheel at the top, now and then letting his head lean on his shoulder. "Harry, look out," Bayard said softly, bracing himself, "you're in the left lane."

"Oh, am I?"—coming awake. "Would you like to take the wheel, Bayard?"

"No, you're doing fine, Harry. I just thought I'd let you know you were in the left lane."

"Thanks, Bayard. I shouldn't be in the left lane, now should I?"

"No, you shouldn't."

We all had a good laugh.

A few minutes later he was back there again. When headlights appeared at the crest of the oncoming hill, Bayard nudged him once more and Harry turned dutifully to the right.

Later, Bayard told me that he had been on much more nerve-racking rides with Harry. Once on a late-night drive Harry had got into the left lane on a straightaway and couldn't be nudged out. Another car had appeared suddenly as a speck in the distance and then had loomed larger and larger, on a collision course. The other driver finally came to a slow halt, bewildered, and Harry put on his brakes a few yards from him. They had both looked out the windows at each other, and Harry had said, "Sorry about that." Then he began backing up and wouldn't stop. A car coming up from behind then had to stop, and finally there was a traffic jam in the middle of nowhere.

Now, going from left to right, we streak into Marshall—first stop, one of Lowney's brothers, to get his wisdom on the situation. He had had some sort of law-enforcement experience.

*

The brother was cheerful, showing the same good white teeth that Lowney had. He called his wife in from another room to have a look at me, not so much for nurse duty as just to observe the sight. "Come here and get a load of this, honey. I've never seen a guy's head look like this."

"Wheww!" she said. A quiet and sleepy-eyed woman, she screwed up her face. "It hurts to look. Aren't you in pain?"

"It's not too bad," I said, not minding the attention. It was satisfying in a way, feeling and showing the signs of battle and being able to carry on more or less normally.

The wife gave me some ice cubes in a handkerchief, which I pressed against one eye and then the other, and I repeated once again my tale of what had happened that evening.

"We may not be enough to take him," Lowney's brother said. "A crazy guy like that can get as strong as ten men."

"Aw, I could handle him with one arm tied behind me," Bayard said. I winced. "I sure as hell won't turn my back on him."

"We've got to get him out of that house," Harry said, holding himself straight, face angry. "We can't have him living there any longer."

"What will Lowney say?"

"We just don't have time to check her," Harry said. "This is my decision."

"Then let's get a deputy sheriff and go up there," Lowney's brother said. "We got to have authority."

We roused a tall, thin deputy sheriff from his bed preparations, and he drove with us to the old Victorian house. His uniform had sharp, military-style creases, and the badge over his breast pocket picked up glints of light. On his right hip there was a service revolver in a shiny holster. His belt had a row of gleaming, polished bullets. His gray Western hat sat squarely on his head. "Do you know if he may be armed?" he asked me.

"Not with a gun, although he might," I said. "He could have a butcher knife. I tell you he is crazy. Believe me."

130

All downstairs lights were off in the house as we drove slowly up, easing into a quiet stop. Upstairs, though, a light burned in Jud's front bedroom. The shades were all drawn. The five of us got out, walked into the dark house, the deputy sheriff using a huge law-enforcement flashlight to guide us, and climbed the stairs to Jud's bedroom. A bar of light showed beneath the door, and no sound came from within. The thin deputy sheriff started to knock, then abruptly changed his mind. In the spooky glow of the flashlight I saw that he was nervous and uncertain. He handed his flashlight to Harry and took out his service revolver. Would Jud be behind the door with a meat cleaver? The deputy sheriff knocked. No answer. Another knock—and I heard a distinct clearing of the throat, and a meek, "Who's there?"

"This is the law," the deputy sheriff said. "We're coming in. Don't move."

He flung the door open, revolver up, and we entered. Jud lay snuggled under blankets, in flannel pajamas, reading by the light of a swivel-necked lamp. Pipe tobacco and ashes ran down the top of his pajamas as usual. When he saw the revolver, his face—I was happy to note—showed fear. He blushed, and put the book down.

"Jud, we think it's best if you catch a train and go back home," Harry said.

"I don't . . . ah-hum . . . have any money," he said, looking from eye to eye, fearful, a trapped animal.

"I'll buy your ticket," Harry said.

"But I'll need more if I have to start from scratch again. I'll have to have room and board."

"All right. I'll give you a hundred bucks extra. Now I think you'd better dress and pack. We'll take you to the train station."

Here, I thought, he gets freedom and a bounty for going crazy. What justice!

He threw back the covers, displaying pale white feet. The others might avert their heads while he dressed—I couldn't afford the luxury. He went into a corner, turned his back, and shed his pajamas. Then he put on a pair of ripped and dirty Jockey shorts. As he was buttoning his shirt, lost in space, I said, "Jud, just one question. Why did you have to hit me from behind?"

He swung, eyes hot. "I never did that!"

"Yes, you did."

"Boys, boys," Harry said.

Did they suspect that this had just been a little disagreement between two people and that Jud had simply got the best of me? Even I had to think back, replaying how a flying fist felt from behind, with no warning. This had not been a situation like those in Jim's book, where people had fought it out to prove manhood, coming at each other head on in mutual anger.

Clothed and packed finally, Jud put on a grease-spotted cowboy hat he had lifted from the Colony's throwaway heap and we all went down the stairs. He walked in the middle and I stayed a few steps behind. He rode in the front seat of Harry's car while Bayard and I took up positions in the back.

The deputy sheriff and Lowney's brother left us in a burst of handshakes and farewells. "Thanks a lot," Harry said to the deputy sheriff. "We feel like hell getting you out of bed the way we did."

"Nothing to it," the man said, jovial now, revolver put well away. "It's all part of my job."

"So long"—to Lowney's brother.

"Take it easy now," as if we'd just been on a social visit.

Driving to Terre Haute, I didn't take my eyes from Jud. He didn't speak, but a grin—the shit-eating one—grew as we sped down a throughway. At the train station, ticket in hand, he pocketed the hundred dollars from Harry, making no comment, rocking back on his heels. The train pulled in and he boarded it with no word. I watched him take a seat next to the window, and he did not look out.

"Come on," Bayard said, "we got him on the train. Let's clear out."

"No," I said. "Not yet."

The train started with a jolt, and then pulled away. I saw Jud's head under the wide-brimmed cowboy hat disappear down the tracks. He didn't look back.

*

I spent three days on my letter to Lowney, giving the details in narrative form, not forgetting the five senses and throwing in a few similes to boot: my head thumping against the radiator like a watermelon being plunked. I had visions of Jones reading the letter and I wanted it to read as well as possible, to reap what I could from being a victim of a behind-the-back assault.

Lowney's reply came back like a shot, page after page, single-spaced. Quintessential Lowneyisms. " . . . Of course Jud has been in a mental institution two or three times. I knew this, BUT IT DOES NOT BOTHER ME. THEY RAILROAD PEOPLE TO MENTAL INSTITUTIONS IN THIS COUNTRY ALL THE TIME. It's a toss-up whether the quacks of psychiatry or the FBI are finally going to take over. Look in the front of your phone book for emergency numbers if you don't believe me. It lists the FBI right

133

next to the one for an ambulance. FORGET YOUR EGO. You will never write until you throw off the things of this world. I HAVE A HUNCH THAT JUD MAY HAVE BEEN GIVEN A RAW DEAL—and that little old lady in the house may be the nigger in the woodpile. That's what we say in Kentucky: Look out for the nigger in the woodpile. ABE LINCOLN WAS RAILROADED IN SPRINGFIELD! Copy, Johnny. We will be back in a few weeks. Jim is writing a hell of a novel, his best yet. This summer we're going to have some books to take to New York that are going to knock them on their asses. Yours may be among them. . . . "

The long scenes that I had been writing—my book—had reached a natural cutoff point and I began typing them over into fresh copy to show Lowney. She had said, "Rewrite, rewrite, rewrite. The best writing comes from rewriting. That's how Hemingway does it." Like "write it cold" the command to "rewrite" seeped into me, although I was a little unclear as to what it meant. I went over copy, changing one adjective for another, adding a phrase here and there, and typing everything over once more. Rewriting did not mean—under the sway of Lowney—chopping anything out. Anytime you tried to spin a yarn in conversation, she'd sail in with, "Get it down! Get it down! Don't lose it, don't lose it!" Everything went in and our manuscripts grew like fungus, not like frail plants that must be watered and tended and carefully pruned.

We did not read books on how to write fiction. Lowney mentioned a book by Tom Uzzell, *Narrative Technique*, saying time and again that Jim had learned from it at one point, but the rest of us were not to touch it—as if it were a drug we might not be able to handle. "If you knew how to handle Tom Uzzell, he could do wonders for you. But if you got hung up on him, he'd kill you. He helped Jim until Jim could think of nothing else and got blocked. DON'T THINK. Let it flow. Copy! Copy!"

And old Mrs. Handy, through it all, kept plugging away. From her small study off the kitchen I could hear a steady "rap . . . rap . . . rap" as her two-fingered assault continued on the old Smith-Corona. I could see her manuscript on the edge of the table occasionally, as tall as mine. "How'd the work go today?" I'd ask, over cheese and potatoes.

"I'm getting it down," she'd say.

And Bayard burst in from time to time, Abigail waiting and puffing in the car, to break the monotony and insure that I didn't work too regularly. (His own writing was not going too well.)

After the lumps left my head and my black eyes turned to light purple, he introduced me to a recent divorcée with fine calves and pointed breasts (an ex-cheerleader), and it wasn't long until I had her cornered in the front seat of my Plymouth. I parked—as a minor desecration—in Colony grounds. Not far from where Lowney used to scream. With the moon playing between shadows that night it re-created the atmosphere I had often found myself in with Juanita. "Oh, baby," I said, slipping an arm around her back and coming down on her mouth.

She wouldn't let me have her tongue, and kept squirming her tight lips away. I had my first inkling that to have been married does not mean that proficiency in sex has been attained. I had thought only the unmarried suffered sexual woes. When you're married, you can have it anytime you want—in bed, the blinds drawn, in privacy. This ex-cheerleader had had a husband. She must know a lot about it. What was bothering her?

My hand went up her pleated, cheerleader-type skirt, and I felt her underwear. In the moonlight I could now see it. It was white and it was torn around the crotch. From daily use, I was sure, not from a groping calloused mitt. She shivered and drew back. "It's no use," she said. "I just can't. I don't know what's wrong with me."

"I promise I won't hurt you."

"It's not that." She looked defeated, palms up on her lap. "I couldn't open up with my husband. With anybody."

The inkling grew as I drove her home—she couldn't, although she wanted to. Imagine that! And she had been a cheerleader, the symbol of all we had ever lusted for. Those innumerable fantasies of pleated skirts going up and crimson panties going down, all in a halo of white teeth and locomotive energy. What irony! She just couldn't.

And then Nelms, the Hemingway devotee, dropped down from his factory job in Bloomington for a visit. He had cash in his pocket, and wanted company for a toot in Terre Haute. He hadn't been writing at all that winter—just drawing a salary and reading Hemingway over and over. As we sat in my car by a curb in the hometown of Theodore Dreiser, getting the lay of the land, Nelms said, "We have a choice. Either a few drinks first and then the whorehouse. Or the whorehouse and then a few drinks."

"You letting me have five bucks, right?"

"As much as you need. Five, ten, twenty. Just have a good time. When you're in the chips, you'll do the same for me. I know you will."

Good old Nelms. "The whorehouse."

It was less hectic in the sealed-in bunker on Cherry Street than when the full Colony team had been there. Nelms and I crossed our legs on the sofa, the only customers, and talked to

the plain, strident-voiced girl who looked like a novice nun—
our madam. It was a sunny afternoon, but here in the linoleum-floored living room lamps glowed as if it were midnight. "Do you ever fuck anybody?" Nelms asked the novice-
nun madam. It was a whorehouse; we felt entitled to say
anything.

"No. Never." No smile.

"I bet you'd be the best piece of tail in the place," Nelms
continued, getting worked up, jiggling his foot. "What if I
gave you fifty bucks? Would you lay me?"

"You ain't got fifty bucks." She spit out the words through
a raising of her upper, lightly mustached lip. "Come on, I
can't jive with you all day. I'm going to call out some dates
for you. You been sitting here long enough."

"Can't we relax just a second first? We ain't hardly got our
breath yet."

"What-a you think this is, the Greyhound Bus Station? You
either take a date or get the hell out." An angry vein stood
out on the side of her neck. *"Jackie!"*

An older woman with too-dark hair—a dye job—came out
from a bedroom in a pink robe that was not too successfully
closed. She looked pretty in the soft glow of lamplight, and
had once undoubtedly been highly attractive. Scuttlebutt
from the Colony had it that she gave fantastic blow jobs,
filled with a playing of the balls, ass tickling, and going down
to the nub like a sword-swallower, no matter the length of
the tool. Such were the legends of the Colony. I noted that
she wore bright red lipstick applied in an arch to make her
mouth seem larger. And that robe did have a way of effort-
lessly coming open.

She rubbed her eyes as if she had just been awakened.
"O.K., who's ready?" she said, and yawned.

"That one," and the novice-nun madam pointed to Nelms.

"Well, might as well," he said. He walked with a slump of the shoulders that had come from lifting factory cartons all winter. He disappeared behind the bedroom door, and we could hear the rustle of clothes and muted talk. A long, long sighing pause. Then bedsprings pounding. Good old Nelms.

"Is she the only one on today?" I asked, being polite.

"Naw, we got a new girl in from Chicago. Ain't learned much yet, but maybe you'll like her. *Jan!*"

In came a button-eyed girl in a regular dress, her thick, dark hair trimmed short. She didn't seem to know what to do with her hands, first keeping them in front of her and then behind her. But there was something cocky about her too, the way she looked right at me. I knew immediately who she reminded me of. "O.K.?" And I pointed to her and back to me.

"Sure. Let's go."

The bedroom we had seemed out of place for us: the zinc washbowl for genitals, the Lysol smell, the cheap yellow bedspread. "Unzip me, will you? I can't reach back there," she said, and her voice was a shade harder than I expected. But just a shade. A Northern accent.

I unzipped her, watched her bring the dress over her head, and then looked at her standing before me barefoot in her underwear. Her nether bush pushed out against her white, sensibly cut panties, its darkness and lushness showing clear. What sort of lingerie was this for a prostitute to be wearing? Her bra was also white and stretched tight with no fancy upswings to emphasize cleavage or fib about fullness. "Take it all off now, will you? I want to have a look at you."

"Do my bra then."

And I unhooked it the way I used to do Juanita's in the

138

moonlight and reflected glow of a drive-in movie. It had the same funny, hard-to-operate clasp—something that made you want to rip it off. She turned sideways to me, quickly shimmied from her panties, and tossed them with a wave to the corner. She laughed, frowned, and wiped her forehead. "Hey, aren't you even going to take off your shirt? I'd like a look at you too."

I flew out of my clothes, wanting now to get past that barrier so it wouldn't have a chance to torment me. Perhaps she wouldn't like skinny guys—or, more to the point, the type of tool on me. Up in Chicago no telling what kind of instruments they had going. I usually didn't worry about these things with a whore.

"Hey, you're all right," she said. "You look sweet."

"Yeah, you think so?"

"Boy, do I ever. When I heard my name called, I thought there would be some fat, red-faced creep waiting for me. Or some white-haired guy with a cane. This is a real surprise. Why are you coming around here anyhow?"

"I'm a writer."

"A rider?" My accent. "What do you ride?"

"No. Writer. W-r-i-t-e-r. [Or were there two t's?] I stay at this writer's colony over in Marshall. We don't get a chance at girls too often, and none of us have girl friends."

"Why?"

"Because the woman who runs it doesn't want us to. She says we have to concentrate on our books."

"Then she does it with you herself. Is that it?"

"No."

"You're kidding me about all this. Come on now. This is the weirdest thing I ever heard. I'll tell you the truth about me if you'll level with me. Are you married? Is that it?"

139

"No, I swear to Christ and hope to die on this yellow bed-spread—I am a writer at a writer's colony, and I'm writing a book. Now you tell me about you. You promised."

She lay on her back, one hand worrying a loose thread in the bedcover. I propped myself up on an elbow, shooting a free glance down her when she wasn't looking. Her legs were stocky, muscular like Juanita's, her breasts perhaps one size larger. Her nipples were pale blue and unveined, unhardened yet from use. I couldn't get over how thick her pubic hair was, a forest with tiny curls scattered about like daisies. A thin black extension ran up to her belly button, like a wire going into a socket. I didn't know whether to be excited by all this lushness or not. Juanita had had a classic Van Dyke.

"My real name is Jan. What whore would ever pick Jan to go by? I guess one of these days I'll call myself Cheri or Candy or something if I stay in the game long enough. O.K., how did I get into this? I just hung around the joints in Chicago too long and didn't have a regular job. I ran up a few tabs, you see. And there's always guys in the mob around to help out girls like me."

"But how'd you end up in Terre Haute?"

"You think I'd go into a house in Chicago? God, one of my brothers or uncles finds out and I'm dead. No, I'm shipped out to a spot where they'll never find me. The mob takes care of you in little ways like that. They're not so bad."

"Do you mean to tell me that this whor—this place is run from Chicago?"

"Why certainly. You think that Concetta out there just got a gang of us girls together and said, 'O.K., gals, let's form a whorehouse'? There's a lot to this operation you'll never see. It's a complex business. And, cripes, speaking of that, let me

140

have the five dollars. You're supposed to hand that over before I undo a thing."

I handed the sum over and waited for the ritual to catch up with itself.

"Do you want me to wash you?" she said. "I know I'm supposed to, but you look clean. Do we want to waste time doing it?"

"No, that's O.K." We didn't want to follow standard whorehouse procedures too closely—else we would lose what we had going between us. I kissed her, lying flat out on the bed, making her take my tongue. And broke a hallowed whoredom rule: A girl can kiss you anywhere but on the lips. She can give you a trip around the world (twenty-five dollars, specialty of the house), from the tip of the toes to top of head, tongue flicking into crannies like an artist's paintbrush, but she must always bypass your lips. Kissing on the lips is sacred, reserved—as legend had it—for true love. But now that I had kissed her, what next? I hugged her and let my hand lose itself—go out of sight—in her furry forest. Then I was pulling apart her legs, as if coaxing a shy teen-ager into it, ready almost to couple. We were about the same age.

A rap on the door: "Time, Jan, time!" Concetta. Our madam.

I rolled over on my side. "Don't stop now, darling," Jan said. "You were almost there."

"It's gone down. That banging on the door."

"Here, let me help. We shouldn't have spent so much time talking." She rubbed me between her legs, wet her finger and did something else. It jerked a couple of times, and then drew back more into itself. God, it's going to disappear. I tried thinking frantically of Debbie Reynolds, Carmen Miranda, and Juanita. Nothing worked. "Won't it go up? We still have time if you can make it go up."

"Couldn't you—you know—kiss it——"

"I'm not doing that. I don't do that."

"But how can you stay in this business if you don't?"

"Guys'll just have to take me for what I am. If they don't like it, then they can pick someone else. Like Jackie in the next room."

"I honestly and sincerely do like you. I didn't realize someone like you would be here when I came. You remind me of a girl friend I had back in Tennessee." I looked down at her wheat field. "Of course no two people are exactly alike."

"Oh, it's so good with you too. I could fall for you. But that sort of thing has always been my trouble."

We hugged. I relaxed, expecting to put my clothes on and leave, and got an immediate erection. It was so sudden that she was not then ready. "We should always keep jelly beside us," she said, "but I keep forgetting. . . . Oh, here, darling; here, here."

A rap. Hard, persistent, and meaning business. "Come on. What the hell. You asleep in there?"

"Just a minute. Only a minute longer!"

"You're losing money, Jan, *money!*"

She threw on a robe, tied the cord tightly, and rushed from the room. She came back to say, "Do you have just a little bit more money?" She noticed my expression change. "It doesn't have to be five dollars. Two dollars, three, anything. I won't get a cent of this by the way. It's for the house. It's the only way I can stay with you longer."

I slipped two dollars from my wallet. No need to go overboard. She held a bill in each hand, looked at them, and then left the room. I could hear her and Concetta talking outside,

142

mostly Concetta. "That'll give us five more minutes," Jan said, back in the room, robe off.

We used every second of that time, but it didn't work. When the rapping came about once more, I called out, "O.K., O.K., you win. We're putting on our clothes. Take it easy."

Leaving the project unfinished made Jan much more desirable, much more to be pursued. I had a vague notion of what I wanted, but how to put it in words—me, the writer. "Couldn't we, say, sort of meet on a date or something?"

"They kill us for that," Jan said, speaking through the dress going over her head. "I don't mean literally. But it's a rule you don't break. . . . But maybe I'll bump into you around town sometime."

"If we could eat a meal together. Something like that."

"They got such lousy restaurants in this dump. I haven't had good spaghetti once. And forget about their lasagna or ravioli."

"You Italian?"

"Yeah. What are you?"

"I don't know. Scotch-Irish, I guess."

"What a combination. Us. Come back to see me." We kissed before opening the door—me to go on to an afternoon and night of beer drinking, her to God knows what.

"I will, Jan. I'll come back."

That night, as Nelms and I hit the cheaper night spots, I kept my eyes peeled for her. Telling myself, she should be through with her eight- or ten-hour shift along about now; she might be going out for entertainment. As we passed movie houses, lurching from beer joint to beer joint, I watched for the slight of her cropped black hair at the ticket window. The next day—hung over and into my novel—I was thankful I hadn't tied up with her, that I probably wouldn't get anything going with her. If you had a girl—God, a true real whore—what monkey wrenches might it not throw in the machinery? Now I was able to sit and type and think only about pleasing Lowney. I was safe. With a girl in Terre Haute I'd be required to shoot over there every day or so. I didn't have any money. And—worst horror!—she might drop by the Colony this summer. I pictured her wheeling up with a couple of girl friends, giggling and thinking we'd all have a party.

Still, it didn't hurt to daydream. I saw her, shift finished, reading a book—*The Naked and the Dead* or *Eternity*—propped up in bed. I saw her in a restaurant, a candle dripping down a straw-cushioned Chianti bottle, breadsticks in a glass, elbows resting on a checkered tablecloth. She was introducing me, the writer from Tennessee, to a mob of beaming and well-fed Italians, good folk, the salt of the earth. And since she was hauling in quite a piece of change from her work, money was no problem. After all, what did we need—a little wine, some bread, the price of a movie ticket now and then? The fact that she was a practicing whore was a plus. When she came to me after hours, when she gave me tenderness, she meant it. No one passing through the portals of the whorehouse had what I had. It was a daydream. And a week or two later, when Bayard dropped by in early evening, I said, "They've got this terrific new girl over at the whorehouse. I'm not kidding. She's young and pretty as hell. Doesn't know a damn thing about how to be a whore."

"Want to visit her tonight? It ain't going to be long before the Colony's open, and we're going to be cut off for a while."

"You know, I wouldn't mind a bit. But remember she's mine. You can have the pick of anyone else."

144

We pooled our money—I had received a recent birthday check—and we had just enough for a whorehouse jaunt and a couple of post-coition drinks later. I supplied most of the money this time, and that was perfectly fine. We rang the buzzer on Cherry Street, gave our greetings to Concetta's fisheye at the peephole, and passed the row of urinals into the glow of lamplight. "You can bring on the girls," we said. "We're ready."

"O.K., who's free?" Concetta yelled over her shoulder.

From the left came a pale blonde in a diaphanous gown, nipples showing through. And from the right, Jan. In a green and red harem costume. It was probably supposed to be sexy. Her toenails were painted red. Smiling, nodding, heart pumping, I took her by the elbow and led her into the same bedroom we had shared before. "It's you," she said. "Give me the five dollars right away."

I handed it over. She flew out of her costume and pointed to me to do the same—to remove my Colony costume of Levi's and Army-surplus jacket. She washed, dried me, and then lay back on the bed spread-eagle. I saw from the harsh overhead light that she had tired circles under her eyes—and she frowned. "Listen, get moving this time, will you? They bawl the hell out of me if I take too long."

"You're not the same as last time."

"I've wised up is what. All I want is to make enough dough to get out of debt and get back to Chicago. I don't want any problems, any complications, any trouble. You've paid your five dollars. Now come on and get your money's worth."

Didn't she care about my novel, how things were going over in Marshall? What could we talk about—the weather? "It's starting to get hot now, you know, and pretty soon we'll

145

be swimming. . . . Umm—that feels nice, keep it up. . . . We're going to have a lake at the Colony this summer."

"I wouldn't go in these crummy swimming pools around here. Too much chlorine. I'll go up on the roof and sunbathe. . . . I need a tan to go back to Chicago with. . . . There, you're doing something. Get on top."

Over and on and up. I wanted to pound her through the God damn mattress.

"Easy now. I don't go in for rough stuff."

I apologized—and came in the middle of my apology. She hadn't known I'd pulled the trigger until I told her.

Later, Bayard told me that the blonde had given him a "trip around the world" on the house. He asked if the girl in the harem costume had been the fresh young thing I had raved about. He said she looked like any other whore to him, perhaps not as nice as the blonde. I started to lie—to say the girl I meant had left—and then changed my mind. How could he get a "trip around the world" for nothing? "She's the one, and she's great. Didn't you like her looks? That black-eyed look and that terrific build. I tell you she's fantastic. Different from all the others."

"You sound like Jones in *Eternity*. Are you in love with her?"

"Aw, no. I got my book."

*

On the spur of the moment, one unusually bright afternoon, I decided to take a swim in our new lake. Each spring rain had sent fresh water crashing down gulleys into the hole in the earth we had carved out last summer and then had lined with

146

old brick and cement. It was miraculous that this moonlike crater—the result of all those torpid afternoon work sessions, all seemingly useless—had somehow used a law of nature to fill itself three-quarters full of green water. It was like our novels—started out of nowhere, filling up inch by inch beyond our control. Lowney said there would be water and novels. There was water, for sure.

No one around. Green foliage rimmed the compound, covering all the bare spots of winter. Little whiffs of wind sent ripples over the glass-green expanse, reminding me of a treacherous rock-quarry lake back home where someone drowned every summer. The danger of the swim intrigued me, beckoned me on. Who could save me if I got a cramp halfway across? Mastering it was what I wanted. Doing something others wouldn't do because of timidity or cowardice. I knew I was never going to die, ever—but I wanted to savor the nearness of it, to know that it was close by. Besides, I'd be the first one to swim the God damn thing. Jim or Bayard or Sidney couldn't take credit for that.

Now to slip on a pair of green, burlap coarse trunks, an item I had laid claim to the summer before. (Clothes often left one owner for another at the Colony; whoever took a strong fancy to a particular piece of apparel—cowboy hat, trunks, jock strap—got it.) Unthinkable that I wouldn't wear anything to swim, even though no one was in eye range. That's how it was done in Tennessee. I tested the icy water with my toe, and then dived in before I could change my mind. Jesus, it almost paralyzed me. I'm the first in! Here I'm swimming just like always, I thought, head bobbing to gulp air, arms churning, legs kicking, and I made it across to the far side where the row of cells stood. Then I kicked off, and returned to the *ramada* side and my clothes. I dried off by scraping my hands down my flesh. It had truly worked, the Lowney method of making a lake. I had swum in it, grown numb.

I was in a storage room where old magazines were kept, looking once more at the issue of *Life* where the Colony was written up, when I heard a motorcycle put-put-putting on the outside gravel, someone arriving. . . . The article in *Life*, which I had first read in Tennessee, had introduced me to the Colony. If I hadn't spied it back then, hadn't been propagandized by its interplay of text and pictures, chances were I'd still be in Tennessee. Had it been only a little over a year before that I had first seen it? It showed Colony members gabbing good-naturedly around Lowney (staged naturally, I later found out), pictures of a youthful Jim and Lowney, and had a romantic and idealized text that told a Success Story. Jim's story. Instead of someone flying the Atlantic single-handedly or accumulating a fortune on Wall Street, here was a man who had done all I ever wanted to do—published a book and at the same time had shown the hometown they had woefully misjudged him.

I had read the article in Tennessee, let it lie dormant like compost in my brain, and then had gone later to the library of the local college for another reading. Juanita had been with me that spring night, one that seemed to be bursting in green lushness, dew, and bird calls. I had read it under fluorescent lighting, decided I was going to ask this unique woman, the teacher of James Jones, if I could join the fold, and then had strolled with Juanita down a narrow, sweet-scented walk. Around a curve and there was the moon. It was one of those unexpected moments—perhaps out of two or three in a lifetime—when happiness makes you nearly swoon, when destiny turns from a sweatbox into a Champs Élysées with all the time in the world to transverse. Heretofore I had never pictured anyone of flesh and blood making a go of it at writing. By a fluke I had had a story about a boy and his dog published in an obscure quarterly when I was sixteen—two copies to contributors, the chance to see your work in print—and after that an unbroken dry spell, except for a short-lived column I had written in college that had lasted until the Dean of Students had gleaned a veiled sexual hint in one (description of a girl moving her index finger on palm of boy's hand) and relieved me of my post. I had sent stories to *The New Yorker, True Confessions, Country Gentleman,* and the *Partisan Review.* Sometimes the same story. I had even sent a play to Mr. Robert Potterfield of the Barter Theater in Abington, Va. Once a true-confessional story of mine (about a girl from the wrong side of the tracks) was held in New York (or the mail service) for over three months. I even let myself imagine that it might be accepted, a miracle that would leave Juanita in awe and relieve me from ever working for a living again. In time it, too, came back, with a penciled message in the upper right-hand corner: "Sorry, lacks conviction." Failure was what you could expect. Who ever made a success at writing?

But with Juanita next to me, the image of the *Life* article fresh in mind, the fragrance of a Tennessee spring in my nostrils, I had said, "I can do it, I know I can do it. This moment I am positive of it."

"I know you can, I know you can," she had replied, jumping up and down.

"And I love you. I always will. Always."

"Aren't we lucky? Let's thank God we're so lucky."

A year later, and I looked out the storage-room window that had never been washed in its history and saw Sidney skid to a halt before the *ramada* on a Harley-Davidson. He took the goggles from his eyes, like an advance scout for Rommel's Afrika Korps, and peered about, making sure the buildings were still intact, the territory safe. Then he cut the motor.

"Hey, Sid," I cried, running up. "Welcome back!"

"Yeah. Hi."

He was a man of few words in his present role. A Colony Vet. He could just as well have come from a Kroger shopping trip as from Tucson. He answered questions in brief phrases, not elaborating. He hadn't had any trouble on the road; no windburns. Lowney and Jim were to arrive in a few days. The writing was going O.K. He listened to my fumbling account of Jud's breakdown, nodded. He grinned slightly at the intelligence that I had swum the lake, didn't ask for details. He had nothing to ask about Mrs. Handy, Terre Haute, or what room he might expect to take over in the Victorian house. We both understood that he, who outranked me in Colony service, would now take charge. I was a born follower, anyhow. "Hop on," he said. "I'll take you back over to Mrs. Handy's."

I held him gingerly at the waist, leaning with him into the corners as I'd been taught.

In Mrs. Handy's kitchen, amidst her 1918-ish utilities, he told her, in slightly more expansive terms, what he had told me. He unbuttoned his black leather jacket with silver studs, sipped black coffee, and smoked a tailor-made, leaving it in the corner of his mouth when he talked. He belched, and Mrs. Handy flinched. She could never quite make it all the way into the liberated state that Lowney desired for us. Sid himself had trouble at times fitting completely into the Jones/Lowney/Hemingway stereotype. Prior interests and roles had a way of cropping up. Once at twilight in the *ram-ada* he began singing—for no reason we knew—a beautiful, clear tenor. It was so perfect—quivering and mournful—that all speech stopped. Eyes turned. It was a romantic ballad. When he finished, tears were running down his cheeks. "Aw, that God damn fucking song, it does it to me everytime," he had said, ashamed, wiping his eyes. What other talents did he have? What hurts, what longings that Lowney never touched or knew or cared about?

It was good now to see his face, a little brown ooze running from one ear. Like the first robin, he brought the feeling of imminent change.

Part Three

Directives flew from Tucson on how we were to get the Colony out of mothballs. We rolled up the musty-smelling tarpaulin that covered the *ramada* screens, turned on the water, and began scouring the kitchen. Memories of the period last fall when we had shut things down flooded back. But rebirth was happening now, another sunny season coming up. The half-burnt logs in the *ramada* fireplace were at the same angle we had left them, the same line of ashes beneath. A carload of mice turds had been added to the kitchen, however, in every cranny including the dishwasher. "We're never going to get rid of all of them," Bayard said. "Lowney's just going to have to find some turds on the premises."

"Aw, we can do it," I said. I had become a Vet somewhere along in winter, and Bayard and Sid did not have the absolute power over me they once had had. "It'll take time, but we can do it."

Then came the day when Lowney's black Buick rolled up before the *ramada,* and she popped out in her field-gray sweat shirt and jeans, white teeth flashing, and a sense of mission steaming. Information followed in the usual staccato bursts as Sid and Bayard and I trailed behind her flapping moccasined feet like lapdogs. She had arrived the night before, had stayed in her Robinson home, and wanted to get into her Colony bungalow as soon as possible. She had spent the previous night with her husband, no doubt. Was the bungalow ready? Yes, it was. Jim had taken a longer route with his trailer and would arrive in a few days. She had some excellent writers coming in this summer, and some fucking good books were going to be done. She'd heard, incidentally, that some local idiot had swum the lake, and she didn't want that to happen again. All it'd take to close the Colony for good was for some poor son of a bitch to go under. She knew she should never have built it in the first place. We were supposed to be writers, not fish.

"I was the one who swam it, Lowney," I said. Even if I got bawled out, I didn't want anyone else to lay claim to the first lake crossing.

"I heard it was a Johnny and took for granted it was one of the local Johnnies. I thought you had more sense." And she smiled that white smile. Somehow it was hard for her to stay angry at me—someone from Tennessee—as if we were both

156

in on a private joke. "Don't do it again, honey, unless there's someone around to pull you out."

Kitchen drawers were jerked open and rammed shut, books were scanned in the shelves by the fireplace ("Somebody's been stealing books, I just know it. Probably that asshole George before he took off for Ohio last fall. I thought his luggage looked awfully heavy."), and a grand inspection was made of the barrack cells. School was about to reopen. Old hands would soon reappear with stories about what had happened during the off-season. There would again be camaraderie. Yet, ticking at the back of my mind like a dental appointment, was the ritual I must go through. I gathered together the white manuscript I had typed up and took it to Lowney. "Here," I said. "Here it is."

Through the winter, as I had seen the pile of pages grow, I had picked it up occasionally and shaken it, proud to feel the way my child was putting on weight. Later I was to see other writers do this same, almost primitive act, just pick up a manuscript and shake it.

With the manuscript out of my hands, away from its hiding place, I had trouble sitting still. I walked back and forth in my room, picking up a pencil, then laying it aside. When someone spoke to me, I had trouble concentrating on the words and making sense out of them. So much of what I had written—handed to Lowney—had been slanted to meet her approval. She had encouraged me to reveal moods and emotions that I hadn't consciously thought of in years, had helped me to write more than I had thought myself capable. Yet something about the manuscript disturbed me, made me bereft. Particularly now that it was out of my hands. . . . The phone rang. It was Lowney. "Jóhnny, you're to come over to my bungalow right away." A bark, a command. Oh, shit, she didn't like it. Now what was I going to do? "It's just perfect," she added, before hanging up. "Wonderful. Come over and let's talk about it. You've got one hell of a book here."

*

She offered me coffee, had a mug going herself, and wiggled around her compact, cozy study. She wore her tight faded jeans that showed no imprint of underwear; ditto, as usual, her sweat shirt. It was always a nervous honor to have a private audience in this sanctuary. Books lined the walls—a more interesting selection, it seemed, than what was in the house library in the *ramada*—and manuscripts and letters and dog-eared tomes lay scattered on bed, sofa, and floor. Her typewriter sat on a stand near the window, a half-typed page in the roller, the lamp warmly lit above it, everything ready to go. "Charley's going to get the last laugh on everybody," she said, juggling my manuscript, telling me about my main character. "He's going to leave that small town and become a big success. Wait and see."

I had kind of figured on killing him off—like Prewitt. "Is that what you think I should make happen?"

"It's what *does* happen. Listen, Jim Jones has an older brother. Jim could never play football like that older brother or do anything half so good when he was a kid. I think Jeff could kick a ball something like ninety yards in high school. Jim had a terrible childhood. But look at how everything is now. Jim's older brother is married, has kids, and is *trying* to write a novel himself. Jim is helping *him*. Here. Here is a carbon of a letter Jim sent him on writing. One of the best things on writing ever written. Take it back with you. Study it. Copy it."

158

I was handed an onionskin that began, "Dear Jeff," and had the standard opening paragraph that compliments someone on his attempt, telling him how close he is to publication, and then going on to spin out what's wrong with his stuff. It in no way convinced me that my main character should end up a Horatio Alger. Didn't Hemingway characters always end up broken or blown up? The Fitzgerald characters never sailed off into the sunset.

"But Prewitt died, Lowney. He never became a success."

"And you want to know something? Jim Jones fought me tooth and nail on that. One night it came to me and I looked at him and I said, 'Jim, Prewitt's going to get killed. That's what ultimately happens to anyone who bucks the system the way he does.' No, Jim would have none of it. He thought I was crazy. Everyone does. We had a fight, one of our worst. We were literally on opposite ends of the room throwing anything we could lay our hands on at each other, crouched behind chairs and sofas like dogfaces in shell holes. I damn near caught him a couple of times with flowerpots. If he hadn't ducked in time, I would have knocked his fucking brains out. Now he thinks he thought up killing Prewitt off all along."

"Yes," I said, trying to appear enthusiastic, trying to be enthusiastic, "Charley will end up a success."

"And live in New York. He'll be the only one to make it out of Tennessee to the big time."

"Yes . . . yes." In the back of my mind I still yearned to kill him off, or at least give him *Weltschmerz*.

"He needs a wise hand to guide him too," Lowney said. "That sheriff you have in there. What's his name? Ollie. Why don't you make him Charley's uncle and let him give Charley some good country wisdom? There are people from

159

the hills who have wisdom like no one else on earth. Like my dad. You need that in your book."

So the sheriff I had named Ollie would now become Uncle Ollie. It didn't sound too good on the tongue, and I wasn't exactly sure what she meant by country wisdom. Did she mean old-timers sitting around on a front porch whittling and saying such things as 'Modern life is getting too big for its britches'? But I hesitated saying anything and possibly showing my ignorance. Last summer a favorite word of hers had been *empathy,* everyone told over and over to use empathy on characters. I had taken for granted that it meant to *emphasize*—yet why was she hollering all the time about being subtle, to make our statements between the lines, to suggest and never tell? You could never run to the dictionary or encyclopedia or inside your own head fast enough to sort out the barrage that hit you from Lowney in any given hour. You finally had to let words and ideas lie in the brain by the shovelful, assorting them by their rhythm and inflection and never trying for exact, precise definitions. You could go nuts otherwise. But finally she told me to use empathy once too often, followed by a plea to be more subtle. "Oh, Lowney," I had said, "empathy. I know what it means, but I'm just trying to get it a little clearer. To put more emphasis on something?"

"No! Jesus K. Rist, no! When you don't understand something, always ask. How much of what I have been saying has been lost on you bastards? God, I give up my home, the respect of all my friends, my *life*—and it comes down to meaning nothing. I may give up. I may go back to my own writing and leave you guys to fend for yourselves. Then you'd realize, then you'd wish you'd paid more attention. *I'm giving you forty-five years of my experience!"*

It was better not to ask for precise meanings then, especially since she had seemed so happy over my manuscript. I wanted to wallow in the giddy feeling of being accepted, of having pleased my teacher. "We've got to get you a title," she said. "Have you thought of one yourself?"—already reaching for Barlett's.

"No"—flicking cigarette ash in my pants cuff, not wanting to ask for an ashtray. It would be presumptuous of me to have a title. This was Lowney's bailiwick. ("I fought Jim over the title for *Eternity*. I think he came up with the idea in a bar. Kipling. All that glorying over men being together, fighting and drinking. It's bullshit. I'm not so sure, even now, that there might not be a better title for that book. But I've given up. The title for his new book is perfect. It's from the Bible. The man running up to Jesus and asking what he has to do for eternal life. He was told to give up all of his possessions to the poor. Jim's title is *Some. . . Came. . . Running.*)

"I don't want to get your title from the Bible or Shakespeare if we can help it," Lowney said, eyes hot on Bartlett's. "Too many getting them from there. Maybe something out of Edna St. Vincent Millay. . . . No, here in Byron. What do you think of this? *Fame is the thirst of youth.* It's from *Childe Harold.* You could call your book *The Thirst of Youth.*"

"It sounds good. That's fine."

"You might end up not using it, but you can use it till we come up with something better."

This was progress. I had a title—Lowney's—something that would allow an impressive quotation on the frontispiece. I pictured a reader wading through this bit of scholarly, italicized poetry before jumping into some Tennessee prose. What was next, I supposed, was to finish the thing it-

161

self. It wouldn't do, though, to just write it. Lowney had told us every day, like a litany, how Jim had once got bogged down in writing *Eternity* and how she had got a large swatch of butcher paper from the meat market and the two of them had outlined the rest of the book. It had seemed such a problem-solving device, having an endless expanse of slick paper to work on with no need to turn pages. An outline was so professional. I had to have one then—as I had had to have a title from a classy source.

The outline, which had page-after-page summaries of each chapter, was whipped up in a week or two and came almost to book length itself. Lowney scribbled on the margins ("Beautiful" "Wow!" "Build up Uncle Ollie more! Could be best character."), and wrote in slanted script on the last page, "Charley will show them all in the end. He will be a success. Marvelous!" And talking to me in the bungalow, having given an editorial O.K. to my outline, she said, "You know, if you cut out the 'shits' and 'fucks' in this book, I bet I could sell it to *The Saturday Evening Post*."

That was the worst prospect in the world. I wanted to write like Jones and Mailer. What would the guys say if I appeared in *The Saturday Evening Post?* "I don't know."

"It's just an idea. But I wouldn't look down my nose at a commercial venture. We need some diversification here at the Colony. I'm so sick of all these manuscripts coming to me filled with fighting and drinking and whoring around. Jesus Christ, you'd think that was all that ever happened to people."

"I'm not Jim," I said. "I couldn't be even if I tried. All I want is to write the truth."

"Then go to it. You're ahead of where Jim was when he was your age. You've got a hell of a book there."

Jim came streaking into the Colony one day at the wheel of his Chrysler, the silverish trailer bouncing along behind. It was set up in its usual spot, water turned on, a canopy lowered above the front door. Ready for summer. I encountered him huffing along between Lowney's bungalow and his trailer, on the gravel outside the *ramada*. He wore his suspenders and his two-toned wing tips, standard items of his civilian wardrobe. "Lowney says you're coming down the homestretch on your book," he said, a fresh, good-humored stare on me—something I'd never experienced from him before. Was he thinking about funds from a new book going into Colony coffers and relieving him somewhat of his Atlas-like burdens? Was he happy Lowney had shown an interest in another writer? "She says it's really fine. Way to go, buddy."

"Thanks"—embarrassed, proud, wishing I could just stop at this moment, a winning poker player checking out of a game early. "I hope it's O.K."

"It is. I can tell when Lowney means something."

"How's your stuff going?"—nearly collapsing, everything spinning, talking to the author of *Eternity* as if I were a peer.

"Aw, O.K."—frowning, turning on his heels. Not an equal yet.

The barrack cells, freshly cleaned and ventilated, filled up one by one as old hands and new recruits buzzed in at all hours. Even I, after a space, was forced to abandon the easier style at Mrs. Handy's and take up quarters on Colony grounds. As a Vet I chose an end cell, the closest one to the shower and privy. George walked in on the dusty gravel one noon, carrying less luggage than he had left with the preceding fall, blushed, said his waitress mother had kept him in spare change through the winter and that he had matured a

163

great deal—could understand now many of the things Lowney had told him. "I was just a kid last summer." The familiar barrage came from his cell as soon as he was settled in, Jones-cum-Faulkner-style pipes before him in a rack, stolen books above him on the shelf.

Perc arrived in dungarees, his bullet head shaven like Eric von Stroheim, seeming to possess a new, ironlike confidence. Before he had left last fall, Lowney had said, "This winter is going to make you—or break you, Perc. You're going to find out once and for all if you can lose all the shit about you and turn into a writer"—causing the blood to drain from Perc's face and his lips to turn blue. "Make or break you. Wait and see."

"Perc looks to me like he may have done some backsliding this winter," an old hand told me.

"To where? What do you mean?"

"Can't you tell? Something may have happened on board ship—or in one of those ports he hit. He's slipped back into his old way of life, something that's more natural for him. Anyhow, something's charged up his battery."

Like others, Perc pounded away at the machine in the morning and dropped hints about his progress at noon in the *ramada* kitchen. "My main character's name is pronounced *Ski.* It's spelled S-k-y, but it's pronounced *Ski.* How do you like it?"

"Fine," I said, feeling it might be a little too precious for Lowney's taste.

His confidence was even such that he plopped a title on his new work (his whole past work having been burnt that winter in true Phoenix-bird style), and the new title came from on high: Shakespeare. "It comes from the end of Hamlet's so-

164

liloquy: *And lose the name of action.* I'm calling my book *The Name of Action.* What do you think?"

"I like it." I did, but I wasn't too sure what it meant.

" 'And lose the name of action,' " he repeated dreamily, gray eyes shining, not about to leave it alone. *"The Name of Action.* Action!"

He was dancing about, fluttering his hands out in ballet poses, singing, "Action! *The Name of Action,"* when Lowney flat-footed her moccasins into the kitchen, slamming the screen door. Perc's fluttering hands froze and the word *action* hung in the air. Lowney looked at him—in total and unreserved contempt—and brought down a jar of pimentos. She opened them. "Perc."

Perc cleared his throat. "Yes, Lowney."

"This new stuff you're doing is worse than your old stuff— and your old stuff was terrible. It's always ego, ego, ego with you. And this posturing is driving me out of my mind. You've learned not one fucking thing this past winter. Why don't you take up watercoloring or some other art form?"

The clickity-clack stopped from Perc's cell after that. Once, after the clang of the "Come-and-get-it" bell had announced a reprieve from the morning labors, troops heading for more of them good old pimentos and boiled potatoes, I passed Perc's cell and witnessed him flat on his back, mouth open, neck crooked, sound asleep. It was a high crime, snoozing during the morning work stint, something Perc used to be on the outlook for so he could report it to Lowney. Now, he himself was dying by the sword. We sat on the wooden benches inside the screened-in *ramada,* swallowing lumps of tasteless food and hearing a perfect set of snores waft across the lake water. Sounds went clearly between barracks and *ramada* now that the lake lay in the middle, an acoustical peculiarity that the wiser ones among us were on guard for. If the wind was just right, even whispered conversations could be discerned from across that green deceptive water. Lowney flap-flapped in, nibbling from a plate as she walked around. A snore began on a small intake, like a carburetor working on a whiff of gasoline, rose to high C, paused, sputtered, and then fell in a dive-bomber whistle. Lowney looked across the water, speared one last bit of potato, and then walked off without one word—something unusual for her. "Who the fuck is that over there?" Bayard drawled, once Lowney's moccasins died away.

"Let's see who's missing. George's here. Nelms. Good God, it must be Perc. I don't believe it."

Someone left his hot potatoes and woke Perc up. Across the water we heard, "Perc, Perc. Get up. It's lunchtime."

"Wha——?"

He came into the *ramada* unsmiling, a red sleep scar across his cheek, his eyes bloodshot. He did not take part in the conversation, didn't laugh at jokes, and picked at food that seemed to mesmerize him. "Lowney heard you, Perc," George said slyly.

Perc swallowed. He and George had a running feud.

It got so that Perc tattled less and less on Colony members, relieved somewhat of his role of company spy. It wasn't that he wouldn't have continued to keep Lowney informed with the minutest detail of what we were reading, saying, and thinking—but Lowney gave him short shrift. "Perc, get out of here," she would scream, dismissing him from the honeymoon bungalow. "Leave me alone. And leave everybody else who's working alone too!"

"It's just that George broke the large jar we make Jell-o in,

166

Lowney. I can get another one at Kroger's easy because the manager——"

"Get out! *Out!*"

Gone was the rolling seaman's gait from winter. He hung over the kitchen sink on KP, staring at the pots and pans floating in scum. He had been one of the original members of the team, around for years, faithful as a collie to Lowney. And like a good dog, he had learned his lessons by rote and without question. He could preach the virtues of copying, laud the wisdom of the Masters of the Far East, and tell everyone at the dinner table the efficacy of his last enema, firing a fart in closing. He also rattled off about how this country was a matriarchal society, controlled and restricted more by moms than by the military. The mothers were crippling and depriving us all of our manhoods. In the atmosphere of the Colony where pretensions and deficiencies were dynamited away and where any kind of confession could be made that substantiated Colony precepts, Perc told of how he was raised among a gaggle of women, the only boy, decked out in a dress and long curls until practically puberty. "The God damn fucking mothers have deballed us," he said. And yet he had traded one mother for another—Lowney. ("Listen to what people bitch about and complain about and say they detest," Lowney had told us. "That will tell you who they are. Words themselves are bullshit. What a person says he hates is really what he is. He wouldn't know he hated it unless he had seen it in himself.")

And Perc, who would have walked the lake if Lowney had commanded, came near the breaking point. "Sometimes," he said, over the pots and pans, near tears, "that woman is almost more than I can bear."

The Colony was his haven, his routine, and his future.

167

Even if he couldn't write, he must be permitted to stick around to discuss the Masters of the Far East and reprimand new members who broke the no-talking rule at breakfast. They say long-termers at Sing Sing have the same terror of the outside and try to devise ways of staying put. Perc then found a sewing machine in town, hauled it to his cell, and began whipping up clothes from patterns. Now, interspersed with the clickity-clack of typewriters from the barracks, came the purr of a foot-pumped Singer. He was quite good at turning out clothes too—or rather, he acted the part of the perfect seamster. As I passed his cell, I could see him merrily pumping away, biting thread with his teeth, pushing cloth gently with his fingers, happy as a lark.

"Hey, Perc, whyn't you turn out a pair of bloomers for me?" said George at the dinner table. "I'll take 'em over to the girls in Terre Haute."

"Shut your ass. You've never been laid over there. You talk about whores, but you've never had one. Basically you're terrified of women."

George rifled large-curd cottage cheese in his gullet, blushing to his fingertips. Perc apparently had hit the nail on the head.

"And I don't want to hear any of you making fun of Perc," Lowney commanded, causing him to go slack and his mouth to fall open. "Of all who have come to this Colony, he is the most persistent. He tries and keeps trying. Throw him in a pile of shit up to his ears and he still comes on. You can't write somebody like that off. He's got a place here as long as he wants. And don't nobody get cute with him."

Perc stayed. Others came and went with the speed of sound—sometimes light. Nelms, who occupied the cell next to me and wasn't known as a heavy-barrage writer, surprised me. He lay on his bunk at night, loose tobacco from hand-rolled cigarettes embedded in his mat of chest hair. He thought there might just be the slightest possibility that Lowney Handy was not infallible. "Who knows what *Eternity* would be like if she hadn't edited it? Do you? I don't. And how do we know *Look Homeward, Angel* is so much better after Perkins trimmed it? I never saw what he threw away and said was no good. Have you? Who the shit is Maxwell Perkins anyhow? There's been only one who's gone his own way and been his own master. He's the champ."

I already knew, but he was pausing for effect. "Who?"

"Hemingway." He lifted up the worn paperback of *The Sun Also Rises* from his stomach, read a few lines, chuckled, shook his head wisely, and returned the book facedown to his gut. "Study his life. Read what he wrote. It's all you'll ever need to know about writing. All this stuff about the Masters of the Far East, enemas up the ass, and the dopey business about women and love is just so much crap. Who knows how much harm she's doing."

"But why are you here then?"

"Economics, pure and simple. I'm here just for a roof over my head and what passes for food. I'll tell you something confidential——"

"Keep your voice down. Sound really travels across that lake."

"I'll tell you something"—lower voice. "I don't want that woman editing my stuff. There are games being played around here I don't understand, and I'd just as soon be left out. I have the distinct feeling that this whole thing—the Colony, everything—is just something between Jim and Lowney and that we're only here as stagehands. Watch that woman. She might not have your best interests at heart."

169

"But I'm almost done with a book. Hell, I wouldn't have four paragraphs by now if I'd stayed in Tennessee. She's doing something for me."

"O.K., O.K."—shaking his head sagely, taking a further peek at *The Sun Also Rises*. Nelms was eight years older, a big difference then. The older writers tended to take the Colony's insights with a grain of salt whereas the younger, more impressionable ones (eighteen to twenty-four years of age) could be awed and cowed, usually in minutes. With an animal instinct, Lowney only needed a moment with someone to determine if that person could be taught to write and live—her way. "The best age to catch them is Johnny's age," she said, making me proud, a fish on display. "They've lived enough to be mature in some ways, but they haven't had too much shit thrown their way. He's got no wife, no girl now; he's not tied to his mother's apron strings, and he's through with college and knows it's horseshit. He's even got the Army under his belt. The perfect, perfect age."

One boy, younger than I, was called by his draft board for military service. He had corn-silk hair, a sprig of it always jutting up at the back of his head and a fistful falling over his forehead. He had a shambling walk, head lowered, lost most of the time in his fantasies. The one or two in the Colony who had read *Catcher in the Rye* (it wasn't on the select list) called him Holden Caulfield. He reminded me of my own main character, Charley Henderson, and I was naturally fond of him. More than that—quite strangely—he looked up to me and even listened to what I had to say. Then it came to me that through his eyes (using the old empathy) I was author of an almost-finished novel, a Vet, someone who should have a wide fund of knowledge if not wisdom. I couldn't then have a heart-to-heart talk with him and tell him what I really

170

thought because he would find I was just ordinary like everyone else, perhaps more a fool than most. No, it was better flinging out impersonal wit at the dinner table, showing I knew what to do on KP, and appearing at ease and not uncomfortable at all in the presence of Lowney and Jim.

And so this Holden Caulfield was called to Lowney's bungalow before going for his induction physical into the armed services. Ways were being thought up to get him disqualified, taking for granted that going into the Army without a struggle was the highest form of frivolity and dumbness. After all, hellfire, books were to be written and the country was to be saved from its matriarchal leanings and its enema-less leaders. A man could get killed in the Army, too. On Colony KP myself, going over to ask directions on the upcoming meal, I waded right into the middle of this Lowney problem-solving session. "And who's to say you haven't got a bad back?" she was demanding of Holden Caulfield. "Doctors don't know their ass from a hole in the ground anyhow. The dumbest bunch of fucks ever let loose on the American people. Say you got a bad back. They can't check it. No, something better. Act crazy. Whenever I want people to leave me alone, I simply act crazy in front of them. Does wonders. . . . Here's Johnny. Tell this boy how to get out of going in the Army, Johnny."

"I don't know, Lowney. I talked the doctors into letting me *go* in. They said I was too skinny at first. I wanted in."

"That's right. Johnny's got this older brother he's always trying to live up to. It's going to get him killed one of these days if he's not careful. But it's a hell of a book . . . we're going to sell it, don't you worry. . . . Jim—Jamie—how are we going to get this boy disqualified from the Army?"

It was always a gift to Jim, presenting him with any di-

171

lemma emanating from the military. Steam rose from his coffee mug, seeping into his brownish, blond-streaked mustache. He grinned, slurped in some coffee, and said, "Tell 'em you're queer." He then jumped into one of those marvelous anecdotes that begins, "When I was out in Hollywood . . . " (Already I was trying an anecdote out for size, seeing myself regaling people in Tennessee with, "When I was out in Hollywood doing this script, I ran into Elizabeth Taylor at this party . . . ") Jim was explaining how this famous comedian, a married man, had told him out in Hollywood that he had escaped service during the war by proclaiming at his physical that he had suddenly gone queer. "There he was naked before this doctor, see, and he says, 'I been fighting it all my life, doc, but seeing all these peckers today at one time has finally done it. I ain't going to fight it no longer. I just turned queer.' How do you like that? They turned him down too. Tell 'em you're queer."

Holden Caulfield looked from one to another, rubbing hair from his eyes, mumbling and blushing. I pictured how he might have looked at home, listening to his mother and father at dinner, helping a kid sister fix a toy. "Don't do what they tell you if you feel it's wrong," I wanted to yell at him. "The Army might send you to Germany instead of Korea. And remember: If you say you're queer then *that* goes down on bureaucratic records forever. Maybe it'll do something to your mind, knowing that every branch of the Government thinks you're queer. Think it all over first. It's your life they're fooling with." But, of course, I said nothing, flicking a cigarette ash in my cuff, acting like a wise, battle-weary Vet.

He tripped over the rug going out, and on the gravel turned one way and then the other before making up his mind. He left the Colony the next morning with a suitcase,

172

hair slicked down except for the unruly sprig, everyone pumping his hand in line—and came back that afternoon. Lowney told us the Army had turned him down, but didn't elaborate or encourage questions. The youth shuffled his feet beneath the dinner table, eyes fixed on his plate, uncommunicative. The story made the rounds eventually that he had become so confused as to what to tell the Army doctors— queer, bad back, asthma, peeing in bed—that he hadn't needed to act when he came before them; he had gone to pieces on his own. Now he was back in the Colony, his chance of going to war lost, except if the nation were invaded and every man, woman, and child called up.

Unlike the Army, Lowney had an inverted way of selecting recruits. Nothing raised a person's qualifications more than the unanimous opinion of others that he was unsuitable, unstable—and—the most winning attribute of all—dangerous. She would never allow the word "talent" to enter into her conversations. No one was ever "talented" or "untalented."

"I can take anyone off the street and turn him into a writer—a bum, the biggest drunk in town, anyone," she said, "as long as he has the faith of a mustard seed and will follow me."

To be desperate, to be at the end of one's tether, was the state Lowney longed to find someone in. And she could overlook faults and aberrations that developed once someone arrived in the Colony—as long as that person was working, was depending upon her (or she thought so) in some essential way. Books disappeared from the community shelves of the *ramada*, the petty cash in the kitchen drawer withered away seemingly on its own, and any fresh ideas or anecdotes that were passed along in conversation were certain to pop up later under someone else's banner.

173

"Steal from us," Lowney said, "use us. Be bastards—that's the only way you'll turn into writers. Remember the quote Jim used in accepting the National Book Award, that it's hate, envy, and malice that drives an artist on. There are no nice writers. Don't be afraid to write about me or Jim or anyone else in the world. Jim is a character in at least three books that are being written here. And I've run across several bitchy, awful women that could only be me. Use us. You see us in action. You're fools if you don't."

It pained her finally that Jud, who at last had revealed a psychotic, murderer's instinct, was not amongst us that summer. Until he had beaten me senseless, she had dismissed him as a writer. Now she expected great things of him. "I have the sneaky hunch that that old biddy down the way ran Jud off," she told me. I had given up trying to explain what had happened. I accepted the fact that I would now have to fight Jud to the death if we ever ran across each other again. "The old biddy runs off all the good writers she can. Jud got a raw deal. If he's not in the cuckoo house by now, he can come back here. I'm waiting to hear from him."

The person who drew the most scorn from her was also absent, one whose cluttered reputation lingered behind. It was Jeremy from West Virginia, a legend. "I made the big mistake of telling him about my own book," Lowney said. "So guess what? He stole the idea lock, stock, and barrel. He didn't change a thing. The fucking thief robbed me of three years' work and the best idea I ever had. It came from a story my brother told me about life on a submarine. That Jeremy. Everytime he came to my bungalow I'd be missing money or jewelry or something right away. The last time I kicked him out he left with the only copy I had of *The Left Hand is*

Nearer the Heart. I know he lifted it. It's out of print and awfully hard to get, the son of a bitch."

"I just can't stand his face," Jim said. "That oily, simpering look he has. It reminds me of Uriah Heep. Or a fresh-laid turd."

"And that voice. That deep, rolling, cultured tone he takes. He thinks I'm ignorant, but I know that his father was a coal miner. The asshole, he's terribly ashamed of his father, someone who killed himself in the pits just to put him through college. His father was a thousand times better than Jeremy will ever be. He lets his mother support him now. That shows you what he's made of."

The last person one would expect to see on Colony grounds that summer was therefore Jeremy. It followed then that Lowney flapped into the *ramada* breakfast one morning and announced that Jeremy was to roll in soon for a stay. She said for us to guard against giving away any ideas about our books and to watch our money and possessions. To the end, while preparing to admit him, she would not say a good word about him. (His saving grace apparently was that he had published a novel, an unsuccessful one. She had a weakness for anyone who had broken into print, still in part a provincial in awe of anyone who had got money from writing.) "He called me up from some bar and started crying," she said. "I told him to come on back—but the first time he steps out of line, I'm going to kick his ass out. And the next time it may be for good."

I pictured Jeremy as I would an unapprehended sex assaulter described in the papers: someone with wild, bushy hair and a frenzied manner. But disembowelment experts often turn out to look like Boy Scouts or Secretaries of State—and vice versa. Jeremy stood on the gravel with a cardboard suitcase in hand, his eyes staring straight ahead. He had a long, serious, Ichabod Crane face, a crew cut; so slim his leather belt had to be pulled to a gorged-out hole that left half of it flopping free. He took a mug of coffee in the *ramada*, asked for and surprisingly received a tailor-made from Perc, and settled backs with self-assurance on the sofa. The Colony Vets, who had gossiped and complained of him most, asked him simple, polite questions, which he answered through a bemused stare. The Vets were too friendly, too polite. Lowney burst in with a mixed current of electricity about her—half threatening, half solicitous. "Jeremy, do you have everything you need to work?"

"Lowney, I would appreciate it," he said, in a rolling basso she had not been wrong about, "if I could use your typewriter. My own skips on me. Also, I could use yellow seconds and some bond paper if you have it."

"The paper is in the cabinet there. I'll have a typewriter in your room by the time you get there. I was going to stick you in a tent for a while, but I've just found out that none of them are ready. Tough shit. You would have loved a tent, wouldn't you, Jeremy?"

"Anyplace, Lowney. Although, to be frank, it doesn't break my heart that there are no tents."

A demonic tap-tap-tapping came from his room, with no warm-up or slow tapering off. Just abrupt silence fell after a while. I watched him walk ramrod straight past my cell, heard the bull-like splatter of pee in the privy, and witnessed him sail back past my door. I forced myself on with my own slow pecking. On the brick pile I squatted next to him while he chipped off old mortar in a leisurely, abstracted way. It would have taken him years, at that speed, to clean enough bricks for the short walkway we were laying. He told me how he had physically written a book in West Virginia. "I set up two empty oil drums in our basement and placed a board from one to the other. That was my desk. I typed from dawn until dusk, and I didn't even need an ashtray. I threw all my butts into one of the empty oil drums. When that oil drum was completely filled, I sent my book away to my publisher."

Hearing that term—*my publisher*—sent a shiver up my spine. "Was it published?"

"No. . . . What's that you're smoking?"

"Pall Mall. Have one." I didn't want to appear too chummy with someone who had the opprobrium of the Colony. I glanced off at other work areas, prepared for flight. But if I could get away with it, I wanted to find out more about how he—a definite, proven, published writer—operated. Maybe someday I could write on a plank between two oil drums. Maybe I could even dare to hope for a mistress in a country-print dress, one who would prepare meals, lie in bed without five dollars tucked first under the washbasin, and raise the blessed floodgates on the current repressed sexuality in me. Here was a man who had taken Lowney up on what she preached—one of the few—one who got what he wanted ruthlessly from her with no qualms, no apologies. He wrote on the outside, could deal with editors and agents and the whole host of people who did business on the hidden side of the moon. Perhaps he could pass on the secret of his strength, his self-assurance, how one could get by without depending entirely on Lowney. But I had to be careful, and go about it in an oblique way. I would give him a hint, an opening, and see what happened. "I don't go for all this stuff about the Masters of the Far East," I said. "Do you?"

"I'm not sure I understand Lowney's complete philosophy

177

on the subject. It's something that's never interested me, frankly. But I respect everyone's religious feelings."

"Do you believe in God?"

"Yes, of course."

"You mean you believe in a personal God up there? Someone who takes an interest in your affairs?"

"I do. Don't you?"

"No." I hadn't had a conversation like this since college. The fact of the matter was that I did pray at times, fervently and irrationally and sometimes with tears in my eyes; but I wasn't going to tell someone on the brick pile. It seemed that the sophisticated approach, the approach I currently aimed for, was to disavow any religious consciousness. The noticeable religious practitioners in my hometown—the Holy Rollers and those maniacally determined to outlaw everything one ever craved, even movies on Sunday—were pests and bullies. It had been a tortured and ultimately giddy sensation to say, "I do not believe"; to say, "Let the lightning strike me dead, Jesus, if you want, I'm going on record as not believing." After crossing that Rubicon, I certainly wasn't going to backslide for someone who was hated in the Colony. Writers were supposed to be above the ordinary anyhow. No one in the Colony went to church; it was unthinkable. "You mean you believe in Christ and the Holy Trinity and all that?"

"Sure."

I would definitely have to try another track with him. "I'm dying to get me a little pussy, aren't you?"

"I never discuss those matters," he said.

One morning the furious typing stopped in Jeremy's cell; that afternoon he dropped by Lowney's bungalow, and that evening he walked away with his cardboard suitcase. "The son of a bitch is not stable," Lowney said. "That's what's wrong with his work. He can't stick to anything. And you know what he had the balls to ask for? Bus fare back to West Virginia and his mother. And like a sap I gave it to him. I'll never learn. He probably stole that Hemingway anthology I've been looking for all week too."

It was the McCarthy era, and we had a token Communist with us for a spell—a curly-haired Canadian in olive-drab fatigues. He was kicked out, not for politics, but for saying "hard-on" in front of Lowney, unleashing the hidden prudishness in her. By my second summer I knew that Lowney was not all the liberated female she set herself out to be. On her own terms, running things, she could say "fuck," relate sexual details that sent you spinning, and talk about the bathroom as if it were the lake's diving board. But let someone else take charge and go beyond the limits she set, and she could pass for a maiden librarian. She commanded that we stop trading with the local butcher because she thought she had detected a leer when he said, "Getting enough meat these days, lady?"

*

The hard core who remained into the shimmering heat of summer began playing group games in the lake. A few, like Perc and George, were terrified of water and only entered it under the greatest of pain in the need to belong. Perc paddled along in a stroke no one had ever seen before, like a beaver, his bullethead well up in the air, not causing any splashes at all. He neither slowed nor looked left or right; some claimed he must be running across the bottom. George attacked the water as he did the typewriter, in a furious burst. As he crossed the lake, he could not be seen, only a

179

leaping foam. He overfought the water, gulping and speech-less after a twenty-yard swim, lips blue and pilfered trunks falling.

Those of us who had encountered water casually and natu-rally in childhood swam and treaded without a second thought. A favorite game was to choose sides, drop a yellow-painted brick in the deepest part of the lake, and see which side could bring it to the surface. A swimmer drew in a lung-ful of air, kicked his legs straight up to show his out-of-date, threadbare trunks, and then disappeared for minutes. Com-ing across the dim yellow brick in the silent, bluish world be-low, ears popping, gave one a giddy, hysterical feeling. We were grown men playing at childhood, almost unbalanced in our newfound fun. And when one of us had managed to get the brick aloft—others churning in a circle around him, urg-ing him on—we all laughed uncontrollably, some swallowing water and going under. Jim occasionally played the game with us, adding a note of seriousness and more competition to it. He had instructions on how to hold the breath and how long to keep the eyes open. And we never lacked for players when Jim joined in.

The lone diving board had great play too. For a while, do-ing a "flip" was the most popular mode of leaving it. George tried and tried to accomplish the feat, but could never quite abandon his body to a suspended circle in the air. He would stand chewing his lip, gazing down the long expanse, some-times starting for a hell-bent run and then stopping abruptly. Anyone could go in front of him; he didn't mind. When he did run down the board, he would duck his head in the rudi-ment of a flip but then just jump in, and begin maniacally thrashing the moment he touched water. Perc got farther into a flip than George. . . .

As a group of us sat in the *ramada* on a late afternoon we heard the *pat-pat-pat* of naked feet on the board—someone was still out there—silence, and then a tremendous, sickening smack. Another bare back had landed on still water, a flip that hadn't quite made it. It was terribly painful as many of us knew from firsthand experience. We ran to the screen and saw Perc's head sticking straight up in the water. He was not moving. "Good Jesus," Lowney screamed. "Have you killed yourself, Perc?"

He could not speak, but he had started to move in a very slow form of his standard beaver crawl. When he dragged himself ashore and disappeared into the haven of the shower, Lowney continued, "I've a good mind to get rid of that diving board! Before we know it somebody's going to bang his head on it and kill himself. None of you can just simply dive off of it the way it was intended. You got to do these goddam fucking flips and I don't know what all. From now on I don't want to see another fucking flip out there. Otherwise, I'm going to take it down myself, chop it up, and use it for firewood."

"Aw, Lowney, it's not dangerous," said Jim, "if a guy does it right."

"Wait and see!"

Jim never did wild leaps off the board, spontaneous cannonballs, or awkward nose-holding jumps. Loins sheathed in a pair of tight, brief, faded-blue rayon trunks, he took precise steps out on the board, jogged high, and plunged straight down in a classic, ninety-degree angle, nose an inch from the wood. Hardly a drop of water jumped up as he went under, feet together, perfect. If anyone were diving at the same time, he took the trouble (requested or not) to point out flaws in his style and how to make corrections. Most only became

181

more self-conscious. "When Jim takes anything up, he tries to be perfect," Bayard drawled. "He's spent a lot of time studying diving and perfecting it, but I don't think he really enjoys it."

Suddenly one blazing afternoon an improbable sight shimmered up by the lake: a blonde in a two-piece outfit that was not only skintight but skin-colored. It was a girl from a local prominent family, who had dropped by to see Lowney because of some minor trouble she was in and who asked if she just might take a quick dip—that is, if it didn't break any old Colony rules and wasn't too much fuss. (Lowney had trouble refusing or coming down hard on members of prominent families, a chink in otherwise formidable armor.) So there was the blonde diving prettily into the rippling green, coming up with a jet of water spouting from mouth and hair smoothing back, and moving easily into the kind of assured strokes that pointed to summers in an exclusive day camp. She sat on the side of the lake, knees cocked out, and two Colony members immediately swam by with heads jerking furiously up as if for air. Whom would she select to talk to? The yellow-brick game stopped, and only the very best divers continued on the board. Surprisingly, she took her body beside L.C., a dark, older man of thirty-four, who had been married and had two kids. He was a fine man, honest and sincere, a good drinking buddy—but L.C.? Didn't she want a younger fellow, a crew-cut, recent college grad? Wasn't that what all blonde, privileged girls her age wanted? We had many diverse opinions. "Little bitch," said Nelms. "Watch her shake that can. She knows how she's upsetting us."

"You can see pussy hairs creeping outside her bathing suit," said George, bringing in the best fact yet.

Jim ambled·by, bare except for sandals and faded-blue

trunks, lowering his great head to pass along a few forced words to her. She turned, mumbling a reply, an alert strained smile flashing up for the best-selling novelist, a celebrity. More dialogue between them, as Jim hit the gravel on the way to Lowney's bungalow, calling over his shoulder—easy banter on the surface, charged beneath. As he still yelled, someone did an expert cannonball from the board, sending a spray of water over her and L.C. and causing her to jump up and shake her breasts for those on starboard side.

"I don't think I'll let her swim here anymore," Lowney said that evening. "She could pick your guys' brains and use it against us in town. I frankly don't trust her. And she's much older than she looks, incidentally."

And then inevitably came the day when Lowney herself tiptoed to the edge of the lake. In brown latex two sizes too small, pushing hair up under an old-fashioned rubber bathing cap that had a bogus permanent wave imprinted on it. Her upper legs bubbled with fat—a startling revelation—and her skin had a rough brown texture. "Oh-oh-oh, this water is terribly cold," she squealed, wiggling her toes in it. "I can't go in this. I simply can't go in this."

"Come on in, Lowney," one after another yelled happily, delirious with the advantage now held over her. "It won't hurt you."

"Once you're in," Jim instructed from the water, snorting, treading, "it won't seem cold at all. What you have to do, Lowney, is go in right away. Don't think. Plunge right in."

She put her foot in up to the ankle, and withdrew it like a shot. "What are you trying to do to me, Jim? Kill me?"

Intoxicated by the banter, momentarily liberated, Perc slapped a large spray of water at Lowney. Seeing her back up, stunned, rubbing her eyes, he sent a second, more powerful one her way. He laughed in goofy spurts, as shocked as everyone else at his aggression. Lowney took off for her bungalow in a girlish trot, loose flesh jumping, ignoring the shouts behind her. It had come to each of us in his own way—Lowney included—that she was no longer young in the way she wanted. A brief quiet ensued, and then we went back to the yellow-brick game and flips off the board.

In the *ramada* Jim paraded about with a towel around his middle, showered, relaxed, expansive, having eyes covertly follow him. He was the CO in an Enlisted Men's Club, sticking around for some uncomfortable fellowship. Possibly he was lonely, too, and couldn't face his trailer or the constrictions of Lowney's bungalow. He told about a fight he had had during the period he was writing *Eternity*. It was at an American Legion dance—and, from the way he told it, I could picture the beer being swilled, the pursued women, the freewheeling raucousness. (Being imprisoned, nothing was so pleasing as descriptions of outside tribal rituals.) A Legionnaire had become incensed at Jim's quietness, the way he kept observing the spectacle, smoking a pipe, not joining in. Jim was not famous then, few realizing he even had ambitions to write. "Without doing nothing, I was bothering the hell out of that guy. He finally took a swing at me, calling me a Polak. The funny thing was he was a Polak himself. Nothing seemed to make him madder than thinking somebody with his own background might be admitted to a private club. It was my last real fight. I knocked him out with a couple of shots. . . . "

Someone else told a fistfight anecdote—a pointless one, meandering, which few could follow. These tales would surely continue forever unless Jim moved to another track. He then began talking about the delusion of anyone thinking he could

184

get reality down on paper, hoping that he could record honestly something that had happened in another time. "For instance, those characters in *Eternity*. I had to give them heroic proportions and make them interesting. In actuality those guys were boring. No one here could stand to be around them five minutes. The real Prewitt was no idealist."

Nelms had a quizzical look which Jim noticed. "You don't agree with me, Nelms? You think you can really get it down? The way it really truly is."

"Yes."

"Why?"

"I know the truth."

"Listen to that, you guys! Nelms knows the truth. The *truth!*"

Everyone laughed knowingly, Nelm's quizzical smile evaporating. The funny thing was, I believed I knew the truth too. Why else think of yourself as a writer? And hadn't I said in one of my letters to Lowney in the beginning those same exact words: *I know the truth.* It was group solidarity now, all of us laughing, in the know, only Nelms left out. "Not the whole picture of course," he said. "But if you select and heighten certain details then you can get the real truth across."

"But if you're selecting and heightening, then that ain't the truth. And you say you know the truth. Guys, when we don't understand something let's just call on Nelms. He knows the truth."

"Jamie!" It was Lowney bellowing from the bungalow. "Telephone. Long distance. Want to take it here?"

"Naw, I'll see who it is first." He picked up the extension on the *ramada* desk we used for writing checks and making grocery lists. He did not sit down. "Hello . . . Hi, Norman,

185

that you? . . . " *Norman*, the ring of that name! Then *Monty* slipped in: Monty was dropping by in a few days. "It ain't out of your way at all, Norman, if you're on your way to Mexico. . . . Norman, Norman. . . . With Monty here too, we'll have a hell of a party. I'll never forgive you if you don't show up. . . . " Jim tucked in his towel a further notch and took off for Lowney's bungalow, screen door slapping, sandals scraping on gravel. Nelms looked at me, I at him. Bayard tossed a butt into the fireplace, and George took on a glazed, ecstatic look. Jim had not told us who Norman was. But he did not have to.

My cell door closed (no locks on them), I took down my battered copy of *The Naked and the Dead.* The jacket had long since been lost, and now the cover on the spine had worked itself loose through heavy service and the yellow binding showed through. How wonderful the memories of reading it the very first time! In bed late, the windows open on a soft spring night, an old curved-necked lamp giving me light. I was a recent Army vet, had learned to like the taste of a few brews in the evening, could inhale one pack of Philip Morris a day, could even jack off before retiring without fear of immediate insanity, spinal failure, or a stigma to keep me from women forever. I turned the pages, tapping Philip Morris ashes into a wooden bowl that had once held Yardley Shaving Soap. He used "fug"—which was close enough. This wasn't make believe. This was how men talked and thought and really acted. The truth. Believing, you could then get caught up in its dramatic sweep—the patrol, the unnecessary mission, the way Hearn caught the bullet in a glint of sun. Every so often, the intensity of enjoyment was such that I had to look once again at this man's dark-haired image, read once more his history: Brooklyn, Harvard, rifleman. His book was giving me the kind of relief and confidence that went along with the ability to light up a cigarette like a grown-up. Norman Mailer had come along before James Jones.

At noon there was a strange car parked on the gravel: a Studebaker with sporty wire wheels. When no one was watching, I took a quick look. There was still an indentation in the front seat. By God and Christ, his ass had sat on that veritable spot. The steering wheel showed palm prints, and I pictured the dark-haired man on the book jacket tooling along with an intelligent, Harvard-grad countenance. I couldn't imagine him stopping along the highway for an Eskimo pie; and when he got gas somewhere, it must have been in such a holy manner that the attendants were left faint. At the *ramada* entrance I caught a glimpse of dark curls, a sharp boyish profile, and someone with hands confidently on hips like a general. He was talking to Jones—not listening, *talking*. I felt that familiar onrush of anxiety and excitement and rapture, greased on its path by adrenalin: the way sighting a member of the hometown baseball team, the Cardinals, on a street corner used to affect me—or, in a slightly altered way, encountering or knowing I was soon to encounter a certain girl I mooned over in high school. My heart banging my rib cage, I knew I could never have marched up and said, "Glad to see you there, man. Welcome aboard." I would have collapsed to the *ramada* concrete first.

But I needn't have worried. Lowney collared several of us at her bungalow doorstep. "I'm sending you guys to Terre Haute today. I simply must have you out of my hair. Go get drunk or laid or whatever you do there. I don't want you back here until late."

Over cold beer and martinis in the nautically designed bar, we compared notes on what we had gleaned so far. I recounted that I had simply *seen* him, a plus but not by far the biggest news. L.C. had witnessed a sloe-eyed, Latin-type in his company, obviously his wife or girl friend. L.C. even claimed to have spoken to the woman, found her dead-panned and of no bullshit; she had told him that she was a painter and that she might work in some still lifes while at the Colony. The whole conversation had taken place around the wire-wheeled Studebaker. It was beyond our comprehension how a writer—an idealized one—could have such a gorgeous and probably talented girl friend, how he could take up with her easily and not be tortured. It wasn't what Lowney had said an artist's fate to be. We fell silent. And then George dealt the *coup de grâce*.

"I met Norman a minute after he came in," he said in a deadly, superior tone. *Norman!* "I saw him drive in, and I knew who he was right away. So I grabbed my *Naked and the Dead* and ran out for him to autograph it."

"Did he do it? He should have told you to go fuck off."

"No, he's polite as hell. I'm not kidding. He even wrote me a little message on the flyleaf, and he didn't know me at all then."

Silence again; hatred for George. *Then.* What did he mean: didn't know him at all *then?*

"He's going to look over my stuff," George went on. "Norman Mailer is going to give a critical appraisal of my work."

"You're as full of shit as a Christmas turkey," Perc said, color drained from his face. "Does Lowney know about this?"

"Yes. She's the one who set it up."

Since we had been ordered to stay away from the Colony, some of us felt for the first time a little uneasy with freedom and wondered what was happening back in the compound.

From the way Lowney had frowned, almost wringing her hands in banishing us, it was obvious that she was going through a conflict. And thinking we realized what her dilemma was, swigging beer in a cool bar in Terre Haute, removed some of her ginger and charm from our eyes. She had been embarrassed to have us around, people who were stuffed with her own philosophy, robots, common soldiers of the movement. Was she afraid of Perc's unnatural way of clearing his throat? Would the pus running out of Sidney's ear turn our guests' stomachs at the groaning board? And was a special meal in the works—one with dairy-fresh butter, thick bread, and champagne? Perhaps Lowney and Jim had a special act on tap for the guests and didn't want us around to complicate things. Never mind the reasons. Just as soon as someone of interest dropped in, we found ourselves in Terre Haute.

"Aw, Mailer's not so goddam hot," Nelms said. "He stole Dos Passos and James T. Farrell blind."

It didn't help. *The Naked and the Dead* was unique, had affected us all too much—had, in my own case, like *From Here to Eternity* and the *Catcher in the Rye,* changed my vision of the world in the batting of an eye and made me thereafter see things differently. Well, at least Mailer (*Norman* now to some) was in our sphere for a short while, even though his coming had sent us flying to the parapets. At the whorehouse, inside a linoleum-floored room with a sway-backed bed and a blonde, I said, "Gimme dat old 'arf 'n 'arf, baby," throwing my privates up to the washbowl. It was all becoming very casual, nothing to get excited about. None of us got roaringly drunk that night—not even technically drunk—and when we drove back in the Colony, the lights were all off, everything still. At high noon the next day, writing stint completed hell or high water, I followed a line into the *ramada* where he stood. Lowney was introducing him—trying to—as if he were just anyone, an ex-jockey or local handyman.

I was struck by the openness and color of his eyes, a perfect blue I could never remember seeing before. He looked straight at you, interested and extraordinarily polite. Usually those who were passing through the Colony mumbled a few words and then closed in on themselves. He had a vast, happy delivery, a certain set of mannerisms that made me remember the intelligent-looking people unloading Wallace-for-President fliers in Harvard Square. I thought I could smell wonderful New York from him, evoking a sense of his writing at night in an Automat, walking the streets before his book was published and knowing secretly that he was soon to unleash a blockbuster. *"Talk* like Hearn," I wanted to tell him. "Give us an imitation of Wilson and Gallagher and Red." But he never acted, as Jim sometimes did, as if he had sprung from his own book.

"Hey, Norman," George piped up. "Want a cigarette? We roll 'em here."

"No thanks. The only thing I roll," he said, "is marijuana."

The trick was to edge as close as you could to him, pretending you were just standing there, nothing else to do, and hear his words. He and Jim were soon on to Hollywood stories, acting out their anecdotes. As one household personality was being raked over the coals, Mailer gave a startling imitation of how the actor talked in people's faces, his spit and intensity flying. And always close at Mailer's elbow, mute, was the beautiful, raven-haired woman introduced as Adele. Such a woman in tow, Hollywood anecdotes, a car with

190

sporty wire wheels—how could he even waste a day or two in the Colony?

"Norman is fighting for his life," Lowney told me in the kitchen, voice lowered dramatically. "He knows his next book has to bowl them over or they're going to write him off. Talk about pressure. Jim's not up against half what that boy is."

The word was that Mailer's new book was about Hollywood. The author himself sat on top of a picnic table near Jim's silver trailer, in mixed shadows from the huge shade tree, reading a snow-white manuscript. He read quickly, the pages flipping over, not looking up or around. It wasn't the style of someone lazily going at it in hammock or by the sea, more the editor whose mind is not out for enjoyment. The manuscript was Jim's. Mailer's verdict, which made the rounds, was that Jim had a tremendous book going, though it might need a little cutting; Jim said that Mailer's Hollywood book was excellent, but that it might be specialized in such a way that the critics and public could possibly misinterpret it. A fantastic rumor went around that Mailer's old publisher was leery of it and Mailer probably was going to have to come up with a new one. How the rest of us hungered for a peek at those manuscripts! What secrets and genius lay there! At the local dump, scattering the Colony remains from meals and creative endeavors from smelly cans, Nelms and I poked around all shredded manuscript pages. "Fly me to the Azores and let me feel cockleshells between my toes," went one line of incomprehensible dialogue. A little farther down the jagged sliver of paper was mention of a character called Sky. Shit, Perc's abandoned novel. Another, filled with obscenity, we decided was George's. On several margins were Lowneyesque notes: "Terrific!" "This is shit—FORGET

HEMINGWAY!" At last something from Jim. Unlike other manuscripts it was on white bond, beautifully typed, at the top an indication of the professional by the listing of chapter, abbreviated title, and page. There were the nouns preceded by three adjectives, the absence of apostrophes. It must be Jim's. I noted that one of his characters was named Frank, an older brother; amazing, the older brother in my book was named Frank too.

All this business about writing must not interfere with manhood though. The subject of boxing came up—Mailer having an anecdote or two—and for a wild moment it was hoped that Jim and Mailer might spar. But something about where the gloves were stored, debate over whether to use protective headgear or not, Lowney's vehement objections, got them off the hook. I remembered those joyful childhood moments when the boxing gloves could not be found, an excuse that left the head intact with honor. There was no reason, though, not to find the trampoline. Its white canvas baked in the sun beside the *ramada*. Jim in his brief faded trunks and thin gymnast slippers bounced twice on it and then did a perfect gainer; he did it a couple of more times, bouncing higher each time, and then he slid off democratically to give someone else a chance. With most of the Colony ringed around it, George crawled on and began nervously going up and down with knees bent like a child on a bed. "Relax," Jim told him. "We'll catch you if you start to bounce off. Just concentrate on going up and down."

All eyes, including Mailer's, on him, face blazing, a sick grin plastered on, he suddenly went into a crazed flip, landing on the trampoline's padded apron on his neck and being pushed back by a sea of arms. "That does it!" Jim shouted. "Get the hell off!"

"But I can make it the next time, Jim."

"You're just showing off. Next!"

On down the line we went. And then there was Mailer pulling one knee over the rim, then the other. He wore an ordinary pair of dark trunks, supported by an inner drawstring that flopped over the top. His skin was whiter than the usual nut-brown sheen of the Colony. He made a joke, and then he did a preliminary leap, his arms out for balance, looking down at the spot where he would land. "How does it feel, Norman?" Jim said seriously.

"Feels great," he said, going higher and losing his balance momentarily, so that arms shot up like a salute. The sloe-eyed Adele looked on with arms crossed and a worried frown. It was always scary at first on the contraption and Mailer was proving to be human. I saw that his big toes had an edge of grime just like anyone else's. He soared higher and higher, coming down awkwardly once or twice, struggling for balance.

"Oh, Norman," Lowney called sweetly, barging up, holding a book with black covers open with her thumb. "I've found a mistake in your book. You made a mistake."

"What's that, Lowney?" he said good-naturedly, on the ground, looking at the page in *The Naked and the Dead* where she pointed. "Here where General Cummings is explaining a curve. It's wrong. The definition of a curve is not that at all."

"It's the way the General thought of a curve," Mailer explained patiently, a little grin working. "It's not my own personal definition."

"But it's wrong, and I wanted to point it out to you."

"It's true to the character of Cummings, and that was what I was concerned with. I won't ever"—grinning, looking around—"take responsibility for the thoughts and actions of my characters. I majored in engineering in college and I've studied calculus. My ideas are not the same as Cummings', a West Point militarist."

"I just thought I'd let you know I'd found a mistake," she said sweetly, snapping the book shut, turning.

"Thanks very much."

Mailer and his lady friend bunked in the rustic brown bungalow near the edge of the lake, a hutch reserved for formidable guests, something like the suite set up for captured enemy Field Marshals. From our cells, we could sometimes see shadowed heads on the opposite side of the lake, passing swiftly by the windows. We knew the bungalow's icebox was regularly stocked with beer, that light bedtime reading matter lay on the night table, and that the amenities went on to include even a private john. (Once when we had gone over a month and a half without a trip to Terre Haute and the Command had taken off for the afternoon, Nelms and I had broken into the sanctuary like cat burglars. We had gone wordlessly and on tiptoes straight for the icebox, putting our mitts immediately on two chilled cans. We then sat on the floor, our backs against the wall, eyes shut and jaws raised letting the good juice wash over our teeth before going down. We drank two cans, four, and before we knew it had polished off a six-pack. We opened our eyes and looked dreamily at each other, shaking our heads, letting out little burps. To disguise the extent of the pilferage we left a can of beer prominently at the front of each shelf. "I've seen Harry nosing around here," Nelms had said. "With any luck, he'll get blamed if they miss any beer." We had taken the empties and had buried them. Harry might have been blamed. We never heard.) Now we wondered what delightful private things Mailer was doing in the bungalow, what kind of New York things was he up to. It was very quiet there, the smallest of sounds traveling across the water to us; perhaps the author liked his snoozes.

In the afternoon I moved through the Kroger aisles, hypnotically bringing in the canned pimentos and large-curd cottage cheese, going over in my mind the actions of Mailer and Jones. Years before, when my older brother used to come home on leave, a naval officer in stunning white, I could only be around him minutes before fleeing to town to glory privately in what a sight he made. It was too overpowering to be around him for long. I had written about the sensation in my book and now I was living a form of it again. Think of it. The author of *The Naked and the Dead* holding back the *ramada* screen door for someone to enter first. The quick, nervous way he smoked. His telling Jim Hollywood anecdotes. I drove the jeep over the Colony gravel at top speed, mind floating, and nearly hit someone who stood with a suitcase. He was in a dreamy state himself, head turning from side to side, lost. It was Montgomery Clift. He had taken the wrong flight and had arrived at the Colony earlier than expected. He wore a wrinkled button-down shirt, scuffed loafers, and the same pair of gray flannel pants he had been wearing in Tucson. We looked at each other, and an abrupt, awkward smile came to his face. The same type of smile I had seen on the screen. He knew he had seen me before, but he didn't know where.

"They're either there," I said, pointing to Lowney's bungalow, "Or *there*"—to the rustic guesthouse. "How you doing?"

"O.K. How you doing?"

"O.K."

As he moved off, I saw that his flannel slacks were baggy and shiny in the rear. The heels were practically worn off his loafers. I could see the beginning bald spot at the back of his head. In a springy step he looked back once over his shoulder and stuck up his hand in parting. I didn't see him again until years later, on a street in New York.

"I want everyone to eat in a hurry tonight and get back to his room," Lowney told me in the *ramada* kitchen. It was my day for KP, doing the shopping and helping to cook. She seemed distracted, angry at some unknown source. "It looks to me that, for once, I should be able to use the *ramada* when I want to. That seems to be a small enough favor to ask for running this place and feeding you guys."

"Don't worry, Lowney. We'll all get out of here. I'll tell the guys."

The fare was the usual: boiled potatoes in their jackets, cottage cheese, and a tasteless concoction laced with pimentos. We left it as hungry as when we started, stealthily scraping inedible remains into the GI can. A Colony maxim was to never take anything you didn't eat: Waste not, want not. ("I don't want to ever catch anybody throwing food away. You can't eat it, don't take it!") But no matter how little you spooned out on your plate, there were always some unsavory chunks of something left at the end. And it was rare not to be hungry at the Colony. Only one dish that Lowney prepared brought out greed, everyone on the lookout that no one got more than his share. This was a sandwich spread, packed solid with chicken hunks and chopped scallions and held together with mayonnaise. The jar containers would even be licked the times we had it, and as often as possible we hinted to Lowney that she sure was something when it came to whipping up a sandwich spread. The ploy seldom worked, boiled potatoes the standard sight to greet us in the chow line.

On extremely rare occasions Lowney would be absent from the Colony, and then we would have to fend for ourselves at mealtime. She was gone the time Jim learned he had just got one hundred thousand dollars for paperback rights to *Eternity*. "I'm going to take everybody out tonight to celebrate, by God," he had said, in the first rush of euphoria. But in kicking around places to eat, nothing struck the right note. It was coming to several of us that Jim, a famous person, might have a weird sight on his hands, leading a gang of cackling, badly dressed youths into a restaurant.

In the final analysis he decided that what he really wanted was to have fried hamburgers and beer at the Colony. Lowney, of course, frowned on fried foods. "We can relax here, men. Let's fry 'em up!" But a problem. It was discovered that no one had ever fried a hamburger before. Fearing a called-off party and boiled potatoes again, I lied and said I had once helped someone fry hamburgers. That evening I burned some of the misshapen patties, left others half raw, all soaked equally in grease, but we ate hamburger and drank beer. "Man, a hundred thousand," Jim said, struggling to swallow a cinderlike slab that had been designated medium-well, "that's a hell of a lot of money. The most they've ever paid for paperback rights. . . . "

Without my saying anything the word had got around that Lowney wanted us out of the *ramada* as soon as could be. Something was in the air, denied us, something that made us want to retreat to our cells like animals. Certainly the meal was nothing anyone would want to linger over.

We began to hear the party and dinner sounds from the *ramada* a little after dark. There came Jim's voice, in high register on an anecdote, stilled every so often by a blast from Lowney. Guffaws carried across the water—Monty's? Mailer's?—and in the summer night air came the rattle of ice, the pop of champagne corks. Here was a soft feminine voice, indistinct and brief, undoubtedly not Lowney's. Was the mute Adele finally talking, now that a party was in swing? Other voices rose and fell—unknown ones, possibly belonging to Lowney's socialite friends. From our side of the lake came hand-covered coughs, bedsprings creaking, and the sounds of George going back and forth to relieve his kidneys.

I lay with my hands beneath my head, looking at the reflection of lake water dancing on my narrow ceiling. I remembered a party a neighbor girl gave when we were both in the same high-school class. At dusk, dressed-up friends had passed, some calling out a greeting. I was shooting basketball goals through a hoop I had erected beside our house, and I smilingly answered, doing fancy footwork and pretending that nothing could tear me away from my goal shooting. No one mentioned the party, just hands flipping up and jokes. After it was too dark to shoot, I could hear phonograph music coming from the girl's house and party shrieks. It was that sort of moment—going in to eat corn bread and fatbacked beans with my mother—that made art and writing seem the only way to cure real loneliness and hurts. And wasn't Lowney always saying that an artist was a Loner, an Outlaw who never fit in? But if so, I wondered in my cell, why, dear Lord, was she throwing this status-conscious bash? Why was she so concerned with it? I fell asleep, and when I awoke much later in the night, the lake reflection had disappeared and the *ramada* was silent.

Montgomery Clift had left the compound before noon chow the next day. Hollywood commitments. Mailer was throwing gear into the back of his Studebaker, face shining and hair glistening. I knew that the moments were running out, that if George could do it, I could too. While Mailer was placing something neatly into his backseat, face averted, I shoved my battered copy of *The Naked and the Dead* under his nose. "Norman . . . could you . . . please . . . "

He didn't need a complete sentence. He whipped out a pen, and in a flourish wrote, "From Norman Mailer, the Handy Colony." Then, his lady friend beside him in fresh lipstick, he wheeled his Studebaker down the gravel and off for Mexico. We waved to him as dust rose and covered the back of his disappearing car. Nothing was ever going to stop a guy like that. He was always going to be polite, engaging, ahead of the pack. I hoped—knew—he was going to pull off his Hollywood novel. (Would that a Time Machine, as he used in *The Naked and the Dead*, have projected me into the future that moment I held the autographed copy under my arm. Would I have believed the fellow who stood before me many years later at a New York party? He seemed to be rising and falling on the balls of his feet, a drink at waist level like a gun. What had happened to them big blue eyes? "I know you," he said. "I've seen you someplace before. Where?" I told him. We chatted a second and I noticed his head turning. He had people to see, rounds to make. "I'll have you over to Brooklyn Heights for one of my parties soon," he said, moving off.

I turned, and almost immediately heard, "Grab 'em! Catch 'em! *There they go!*" The fellow I had just been talking to was throwing punches at another man, both of them circling in a near dance out the door. They were separated and the party continued, my friend acting as if nothing unusual had happened, hardly winded, taking up his drink where he had left off.

A few minutes later the cry went out again, "Stop 'em! Jesus Christ, they're going to kill each other!" This time they ended up nearly tumbling off a hallway banister, a tall man in a tweed jacket working his way between them just in time and talking softly.

At a late hour that night I passed the hallway and saw two men wrestling and exhaustedly pummeling each other on the floor. No one else from the party noticed or seemed to care by this time. If I could have entered the Time Machine at the Colony and been shown this scene, I would have had trouble grasping it. I might have projected that I would have crashed such a party, but that's all. I would have sooner said I would one day wear a monkey suit and work for the Department of State.)

*

The brick paths all laid, a new project was thought up to keep us busy in the hot, nonwriting afternoons. Harry designed a storage cellar—something like a bomb shelter—to be constructed on the hillside toward Mrs. Handy's, the spot where Perc had landed that day on the runaway motorcycle. I struggled with a wheelbarrow full of cement, down an incline of boards, watching my shoes as if they were attached to someone else's feet. Those Bostonians! At one time they had carried a high gloss, nearly dripping in brilliance, the nights I had gone to pick Juanita up. Now they were caked with dirt and flecks of wet cement. The stitching had torn around the sides, and one heel was flopping. At first, in the Colony, I had protected the shoes and not worn them to labor in. But breaking the rule once, letting dust settle over them one afternoon on the brick pile, I slipped imperceptively into letting them go.

Harry, in plaid Bermudas, snow-white T-shirt, the black cigarette holder jutting from the side of his mouth, stood weaving on the hill, overlooking the result of his architectural brainstorm and giving mumbled suggestions. "Throw in dirt behind those cinder blocks," he said. "Gives installation. Keep temperature even all year. Walls sturdy as Gibraltar."

"Hear that, you guys!" Lowney screamed. "Dirt behind the cinder blocks!"

Like our novels, Lowney had elaborate expectations for the hillside cellar. We wouldn't need refrigeration once it was in use. We could save money by buying supplies in huge bulk, storing them there all year round. Any ideas on how to save money were immediately latched on to. No matter how much they cost. Jim had thoughts on keeping a permanent wine stock, the image of choice bottles being brought out on special occasions especially appealing; of course all that under lock and key. We would always have fresh apples to gnaw on. Lowney would "can" in the summer, doing away forever with the need to call on Kroger's for tinned goods. In enthusiastic moments Jim himself would take a turn at the cement wheelbarrow. Not for long, but enough to show he was still one of the guys; like the Pope donning sackcloth for one day out of the year.

"Time for a break," Bayard called, in his role as labor boss.

The unit pouring dirt behind the cinder blocks threw their wheelbarrows over; those digging dirt for a floor bed pitched their shovels away; my mortar and cement crew dropped everything in the center of the half-finished structure. At the top of the hill Lowney sat, knees up, holding her flared skirt against the back of her legs, an overseer. Harry would not sit, hands behind his back, a master builder who did not take ordinary breaks. We could see Lowney pointing to the structure, apparently giving Harry some thoughts of her own on the construction.

Just then it happened, with a quiet *whoosh,* the newly erected walls of cinder block fell in slow motion, ending in a growl of splintering wood and cracking cinder blocks and tons of cascading dirt. An A-bomb mushroom of dust rose, covering those at the top of the hill. As the air cleared, Harry could be made out first. He seemed frozen. Lowney was racing to the rim of the disaster and back higher on the hill and then down again. She was screaming. "Anybody in there? Anybody *trapped?*"

We counted; all safe. Then it struck us. If Bayard hadn't chosen this moment for a break, some of us would be dead. It was that close. Dirt should never have been poured behind the cinder blocks. It had not only insulated but had broken the very back of the structure. Harry still hadn't moved, and his white T-shirt had turned reddish from the dust.

"All here, Lowney," Bayard called merrily. "No one crushed."

She peered down at the jumble of mortar and split wood and cracked cinder blocks where she had dreamed of storing all those canned goods. She suddenly looked old and very tired. "Take off, you guys. Go to Terre Haute. Bayard, take money out of petty cash so that everybody will have enough."

*

Driving away, we passed the shell of the grand house Jim was having built behind Lowney's bungalow. Soon he would be out of his silver trailer, three years after he had become a best-selling novelist. A local builder—the one who rode motorcycles—had charge of putting it up, Harry not allowed to shoulder the whole architectural burden. Lowney relished showing people through the unfinished domicile—old friends, family, strangers, even Colony members who were doing some of the work on it. "Up here," she would flute, "Jim will have his gun-and-knife collection. Over there, on the loft, will go his bed. He'll be able to look right down into the fireplace. Ain't it going to be something? His workroom will be here." (The writing room seemed the most out of the way and unnecessary of all the rooms.)

For a day or two after the cellar cave-in, Lowney's empire-building was dampened. But then she bounced back, as usual, with increased compensating vigor. A *new* cellar would be designed, *no* dirt behind the cinderblocks this time! Jim's house was going to be a beauty, no doubt about it; he was going to have *everything* he ever wanted; she'd see to that. As some of our books crept toward completion, Lowney's mind raced with plans. What she said she wanted was for us to be one big happy family, depending upon each other, and looking out for one another.

She called me over to her bungalow one morning unexpectedly, making me happy that I had a reason to stop work.

"John, you have a hell of a book going. Now you've got to think about what you might do if you come into a lot of money. Right now is the time to think of it, not tomorrow. Jim would have saved himself a tremendous lot of headaches if he'd thought ahead. Now "—laying out a diagram of the Colony before me—"there's this space we own up the road

203

from where Jim's place is being built. What I have in mind, what I'd really love, is for you and Sidney to build a house there. Right here."

"Together? Share a house?"

"Yes. Exactly. Sid's almost done with his book—and, incidentally, it's going to knock 'em dead—and he should move into better quarters. The two of you would *save* money building together. Joint ownership. I think that's what you should do with your money."

I did not go back to the typewriter that morning, or the next morning. All I could see before me was Sidney's head, the way his sparse blond whiskers came out like a cat's, the ear trouble he had that caused a brown gluck to ooze from it. When I tried to picture a ghostly house, both of us with matching keys, I became faint. Did Lowney perhaps have a sadistic strain and realize what effect this was having on me? She began sentences, "When you and Sid have your house, I want . . . " and things would blur before me.

And then Sidney left suddenly one morning, seen no more. Lowney made the announcement at noon chow: "Sidney couldn't take it any longer," she began quietly. "And it's better for him to leave, I think, the state his mind's in. He's only three or four pages from finishing his book, but he has it in his head to shove. Let him"—voice rising—"let him leave after I've nursed him along for years! One of my oldest boys. He's got his book almost wrapped up. So now he decides that it's time he's had enough of the Colony. And you want to know something? *I don't think he's got the stuff to write those additional pages and finish his book!*"

Now the dream house was all mine for a while. "When *you* build your house up from Jim's, I want . . . " Later on it became, "When you and Bayard build your

204

house . . . you two get along fine, so there's no reason . . . " I wasn't daydreaming of houses. I was thinking instead of pretty girls on soda-fountain stools, of walking alone on beaches, of just being able to drink a cup of coffee alone in a café.

Going off course in my novel, I wrote a long scene about a man (the homespun-philosopher sheriff Lowney was always harping on) going off on a get-away-from-it-all vacation. I described in great detail his lying back in a bathtub, sipping on a perfect martini and knowing there was plenty more where that came from, wondering if he should do a little gambling that evening, or put the boots to a one-hundred-dollar-a-night broad, or both.

"John, this has nothing to do with your novel," Lowney said. "A rural sheriff don't act this way. Look at my father, study him. There is a world of material there if only you would listen to me."

Escape! It cried out in everything I saw, touched, smelled, or heard. An editor-publisher of a small weekly newspaper (a seemingly perfect setup for anyone in his right mind) drove into the Colony one evening in a station wagon and announced to Lowney that he wanted to write *art* above all else. He had a wife and child, but he was willing to let them fend for themselves for as long as it took. He would do anything Lowney told him, would sacrifice everything for art. He sat on the porch steps of Lowney's bungalow, puffing a pipe, rocking on one cheek of his rear end as if to favor a case of editorial piles.

"The son of a bitch just may be crazy enough to write," Lowney announced later. "I know he acts like a silly asshole, but you never can tell. Anyone willing to chuck it all must have something. I'm going to find out what."

The editor-publisher had moaned about the coverage he had to give tea parties, the search for lost cats, and golden-wedding anniversaries. But he was a little proud, he'd have to say—smiling a little, rocking on that lone cheek—of his editorials. Of course they made some of the local citizens mad—but that's what he liked. Controversy. He'd send Lowney a couple of his editorials . . .

We heard her screaming on her front porch, holding a newspaper clipping. It was one of the poor man's editorials. Headline: How We Go for Debbie Reynolds. "Just listen to this shit," she wailed. "I think I'm going to give up. Give up, give up. Go back to my own book and forget trying to teach anyone. This is what I get. *This shit.*"

The editorial told about how much rollicking good fun it was to watch Debbie Reynolds, how she always appeared in movies that told stories, and that her style was in a lasting American genre.

"Listen to that! It makes you want to puke. Any guy who'd go for that cutesie-pie bitch don't know his ass from his elbow. That's what's wrong with American males. And anybody who *goes for* Debbie Reynolds sure as shit don't belong in this Colony!"

My heart held a terrible secret, something wild horses couldn't drag out of me. It was so shameful that I couldn't even hint at it in conversation, send out feelers to see how others might feel. It was that if I had a choice between Marilyn Monroe and Debbie Reynolds, I'd choose the latter. Shoot me, call me perverted, never again take seriously a line I write—but it's true, Lowney, true. I'd rather put the boots to Debbie. Was it her white bobby socks, the fact that she was occasionally seen in a living room or kitchen and wouldn't be out of place rocking on the old front porch swing? I was terribly ashamed of this desire because our spokesman for Womanhood, my Svengali, had told me this type of woman was the most evil, conniving, two-faced creature on earth. My memories of Juanita, who looked a little like Debbie Reynolds, became scattered in my brain after lectures from Lowney, the most persistent, hard-to-kill thought—locked as I was mostly in a six-by-ten cell—about how she looked nude and what she said then. The actual, real live women I saw in operation these days bounced up and down on Cherry Street beds and gave their hearts to five-dollar bills.

"Johnny, come here," Lowney screamed, waving my latest chapter above her head. "Your women, they all sound alike now. Your waitresses, co-eds, even this housewife. They all sound like whores. Most women don't sound and think this way. Have you only known whores?"

Was she trying to tell (or teach) me something about women that night I sat across from her in the bungalow, flicking cigarette ashes in my pants cuffs and wishing I were over in the *ramada* spinning yarns with the guys? She lay back on her sofa—one of the few times I ever saw her lying back relaxed—and she fixed me with those enormous dark eyes, which must have been bewildering and affecting men since she was a little girl. Her nipples showed beneath her sweat shirt as always, and in addition, for the only time I ever saw, the cloth had worked up to reveal a few inches of bare stomach. It was a mahogany color, shading off into intriguing darkness at her blue jeans. I saw her belly button.

"Johnny," she said softly, "I've never lived. I'm telling you a secret no one else knows. In my whole life I've never lived as I'm capable. What do you think of that?"

"Shoot, Lowney, you've lived." What if Jim should come

busting in? What then? What if George was up in a tree, peeking through the window, as I didn't doubt he did? "I'm sure you have."

"No"—so softly for Lowney—"I'm waiting for somebody to make me finally live."

"Aw, you'll live. Wait till . . . all the houses are built. You can take it easy then."

"Sure, sure," she said, sitting up, a white smile blossoming. "What my writers need is more experience. I'm sick of all this immaturity. I should kick half the people out who are here, and force them to learn the hard facts of life. But you're doing fine"—seeing me to the door. "Keep copying; I can't stress that too much."

And her unlikely softness was there for a while the morning she left for New York to show some of our manuscripts to the publishing world. She wore a hat with veil, hose and high heels, her backside so firm and sawed off that she must have been encased in a cast-iron corset. She looked very womanly, clutching an armload of folders and loose paper to her now-brassiered breasts.

"Boy, you look real nice, Lowney," someone said, making a smile jumped up from her.

"Wow, wow," Perc said, strutting up, giving an embarrassing wolf whistle that caused heads to be averted.

I racked my brain for something appropriate to say, something fine to send her off on her mission. I finally came up in a rush with: "If I were a New York editor and you came in looking that way, I'd buy everything you had without reading it."

"Isn't he sweet? My boy from Tennessee. God knows we may be related." Barreling into the convertible, pages fluttering left and right, which hands immediately fought to pick up for her, she protested one final time: "This is the last trip in the world I want to make. I'd rather have the Colony for one day than the whole of Manhattan for twenty years. But *they* keep demanding I go there and show 'em some manuscripts. *They* think I've been bullshitting about turning out writers here. *They* think I haven't got a page to show. Well, I'm going to fool them. But, Christ, how I despise and dread the whole of New York City, top to bottom."

She returned from her trip, still clutching a load to her bosom, a page still occasionally fluttering down to be retrieved by obliging hands. She had words for all whose talent had been on display. "George, they're mighty impressed with your stuff. Bowled them over." On and on down the line, till: "John, they liked your first chapters at Random House. One old man in particular. I think he edited Sinclair Lewis at one time. But they outvoted him there. Don't worry, though. I ran across a nice quiet agent who may be just right for you. We're going to sell that book." A running commentary on New York through the *ramada,* on the gravel, still going full blast in her bungalow. "And *they* stole one of my manuscripts. I don't know whose. I can't think of which one. But I know I left here with *eight* manuscripts. I come back with *seven.* "

No one admitted to being deprived of a manuscript, but she persisted. "*They* stole it off me in one of the houses. I can't remember which one. I carried these manuscripts around with me from place to place, right up and down Madison Avenue, and I didn't trust letting them out of my sight for very long. But *they* managed to steal one off me despite that. Now don't tell me they didn't. I know they did!"

Ultimately we were like dogs in kennels. When our masters thought we had been cooped up too long, we were let out to play. If our masters were in a playful mood themselves, then they might run through the motions of the game itself. Yet they were always the ones to hold the hoop and throw the ball; we were the ones to salivate at the chow bell gong. Our masters' moods, we learned, were all important. "Lowney's on the warpath," sounded, and we felt the animal instinct to hide in our kennel cells.

"Boy, you're lucky to be in that Colony," an outsider would often say. "You're supported and taught how to write at the same time. They must be terrific people. What do they get out of it?"

None of us ever knew what they, our masters, did get out of it. At times Lowney—in alienating publishers and editors, losing manuscripts, and sabotaging everyone's self-confidence—seemed to be trying to keep us *from* being published, to keep us forever us in a learner's state, perennial boys trying to please the headmaster, and graduate. To observe Lowney very long was to know that there was for her—when the chips were down, everything said and done—only one.

"He was my first student," she would say, in moments of great weariness or depression. "He came to me first. He is the very best of all of you and he always will be."

Once Nelms came upon Lowney reading a manuscript Jim had just turned over to her. Usually the epitome of the cynic, Nelms reported this time: "I never saw her act that way before. Never. She seemed so tender. She said, 'Jamie . . . Jamie . . . This is so fine, wonderful.' Tears were in her eyes. Can you believe that? From Lowney over someone's work? They must really have something going." The cynic dies hard, though; he added, "Can you imagine her saying that to Perc about his prose?"

We never knew when our masters' anger would be turned against us. Like dogs we might run to them, frisky, wanting to be petted—and find ourselves being beaten because they were in a bad mood. Things had a way of happening between them, things we knew nothing about, that would cause them to lash out for no reason we could understand.

One hot, dry afternoon, that only a summer in the Midwest seems to hold, Jim and Lowney took off for a short respite into air-conditioned civilization—Jim in his two-tones, Lowney in a dress, holiday attired, all smiles. Some of the Old Boys thought it might be a good time to do a particularly backbreaking chore that was hanging over our heads: dig out a hole in the back of Lowney's bungalow to be used for pouring the foundation for a back porch, a pet project of Lowney's. We could really surprise Lowney and Jim by having the job all done, no need to worry, and additionally, by doing it now, we wouldn't be made nervous by their hovering presence and directions.

We worked steadily with shirts off, shovels flying, and wheelbarrows creaking. At the end, a perfect rectangular hole gaping up at us, we felt we deserved a pitcher or two of ice-cold lemonade. We had enough lemons, but soon we ran out of ice. That was when someone—an Old Boy—took the responsibility of getting ice from Lowney's bungalow. He refilled the trays carefully with water, saying, "It'll freeze back up by the time they return. They'll never miss it."

They returned earlier than we thought. In the *ramada* we heard tires skid on the gravel (a bad sign), muffled voices, and then the bungalow's screen door snap shut. In about the time it takes for one long anguished swallow, Jim had charged in on us, face beet-red, Lowney a step behind.

"All right, who stole the fucking ice!"

"We—I mean, I—" The Old Boy was stammering, standing and looking around for help that wasn't breaking its neck in coming.

"I see. You just barged in and took it. We leave for a few hours and already you take charge of everything." (Leave a dog alone in the house and already the little bastard's do-dooing on the floor.) "I've sunk a piss pot full of money into this Colony and I can't even expect to have *ice* for a drink when I come in. I'm sick. Disgusted. I wouldn't mind just kicking you all out and being done with you. If Lowney didn't want you here, don't think I wouldn't either!"

"You broke into *my house, my things,*" Lowney screamed. "Who gave you permission? Who did? I want to know!"

"I—we—hot—thought you weren't coming back so soon, you wouldn't mind——"

"I give up. Give up, give up! Take off. Go to Terre Haute or wherever your vile instincts take you. Only get out of here for a while and let us have something to ourselves for a change. I don't want to see any of you in a half hour's time."

She gave us twenty-nine minutes too much. Colony members crammed into my Plymouth, I raced down the escape hatch. This time the vision of Terre Haute seemed too tame. We were going all out, all the way, maybe even to stay out all night and the next day. By God, we were going to Chicago! "Calumet City is close by," the Old Boy who had filched the ice said, in the first bar we hit along the highway.

"Lots of whores there."

"And gambling. And bars that never close. Shit, we may never come back."

On up the highway, stopping at another bar whose neon looked promising. Nelms sat shaking his head, amused and cynical as ever. "Man, did you ever in your life see the way they flew off the handle. How anybody can write a book around here is beyond me. I think I'm about ready to clear out of the Colony for good."

"She's getting worse," the Old Boy said. "When I first came to her four years ago, she was a lot different. You wouldn't believe how she was then."

It always amazed me how Colony members—especially those most mistreated and degraded—would rhapsodize over Lowney. It was: Lowney said this, Lowney did that . . . Lowney, Lowney. As if their lives were pale spin-offs from her own. And what did they get? Someone who took total charge of them and dictated a complete philosophy they had to live under, not only on how to write but even how to have a bowel movement, as if they were medieval servants under an all-powerful church. It wasn't the brief, capricious moments of kindness she showed them at times, surely. She called Perc "Percival" occasionally and kidded with him. She gave me two red sleeping pills once when I had a wisdom tooth pulled, frowned, and felt my cheek for fever. Yes, in my own way, I was just as much under her spell. Seeing others under her complete influence and being amazed by their fervor, did not make me immune. What she had said about women and politics, Ernest Hemingway and copying, found a fertile virgin field in my unused Tennessee mind. . . . Tomorrow, next day, sometime we would be back under her wing. Now, free and on to Chicago, we would have our moment of fanciful, below-stairs revenge, something of a Black Mass. Greasy French fries, a round of

213

drinks always on the way, a couple of six-packs to go when we hit the road.

"Fuck the Masters of the Far East," Nelms said, in ultimate blasphemy. "Bunch of loony shit if I ever heard it."

"And to hell with enemas," Perc suddenly screamed. He had been on martinis, and now a near-hysterical expression covered his freckled, blue-pale skin. It was the same look he had had when he had splashed Lowney at the lake, giddy to almost insanity with the repressed hostility flowing out and finding the world didn't end. "My asshole can't take it no more!"

Now that Perc had joined the chorus, the stops were out. As the acknowledged Colony stool pigeon, he couldn't well tattle on us after *that.* On to Chicago! Calumet City! We had miles and miles to go, but temptation called in every neon-draped cathedral along the way. What curving nylon-sheathed legs might be crossed on a barstool in this one, or that one just up ahead. We're free, might as well peek and see. At one well-lit bar I noticed that someone was missing. Perc. "He's passed out in the car," someone said. "We'll wake him in Chicago."

Farther up the road, well into the night, the person who had reported Perc konked out was himself discovered missing. We found him dead to the world in the front seat, Perc in the back. Soon the others dropped off, Nelms the last to sag and fall. "Don't worry, Johnny me boy, we'll make it to them bright lights of Chi yet," he said. "Just want to lay me old head back for a little snooze first."

Peculiarly I felt no effect from the barrels of alcohol, nothing. Perhaps it was having to stay behind the wheel and concentrate. If life in Tennessee had taught me anything, it was how to drive while drunk: Go slow and keep your eye on the dividing line; trust that your car, like a good horse, will take you where you wanted to go. Before I ventured into a bar now, I locked the guys in the car, cracking the windows a bit for air. Perc snored, as usual, his mouth open; the Old Boy, I saw, slept with one eye spookily open, as if watching me lock them in, but too paralyzed to protest. In a beery-smelling bar, a shimmering 1930-ish globe turning above an enormous dance floor, I jitterbugged with a smiling woman, trucking on down. Then back to the macadam parking lot, unlocking the car, shoving an inert body over, and moving on.

By the time the bars closed, I saw that we weren't even halfway to Chicago and perhaps on the wrong road. It seemed pointless to continue on with a death ship, heads lolling like rag dolls' as the car bounced and turned. The only place to go, then, was back. Instead of bars to stop in on the return, I tried all-night diners, looking for I knew not what by then. I played old songs on jukeboxes, tunes I associated with Juanita, nursing coffee and lighting yet another tailor-made for my raw throat.

It was dawn when I drove back onto Colony gravel, the idea of Chicago seeming preposterous now. I shook all of my cargo, slapped one or two, but could rouse no one. When I awoke in my bunk a few hours later—brain still triggered for an early-morning rising—I saw that everyone had miraculously vanished from the car. Jim was walking along a brick path, holding a cup of coffee, heading for Lowney's bungalow. From the set of his shoulders, his step, I could see he was in a good, early-morning mood. It was, once again, important to note his and Lowney's moods.

*

The mornings had a new chill to them, a portent of fall. Apples were now a part of Colony diet, gifts from Lowney's country friends and relatives, a further notice of the approaching season. And colds made the rounds, a symphony of hawking and spitting and sneezing. In midafternoon, after chores and before dinnertime, I eased over to Lowney's bungalow and said to her, "All right if I take my car out for a spin? Needs driving."

No one had ever told me to ask her. But then no one ever left Colony grounds without a specific mission: a biweekly haircut, Kroger shopping, mail pickup, an errand for Lowney. She always answered my car-driving request with what I took to be a note of exasperation: "It's all right." Did she want me to roar off on my own, without permission, showing I had gumption? It was another case of my not knowing what was expected of me.

I drove along the St. Louis highway, radio blaring, alone, flipping cigarette ashes out the window. God, how wonderful it would be to do this anytime, without having to ask permission! My final treat before heading back was to stop in a drugstore and have a Coke, savoring the smells and the free and simple ways of the people inside. I thought, in comparison with others at the Colony—even Jim—that I was coming along wonderfully with my book. To every new arrival Lowney had said, "Look at this boy here. He came to me only last summer and now he has a novel practically written. A fine one. You can do it, too, if you do exactly what I tell you."

I was leaving Lowney's bungalow, having brought her the day's mail—*her* big treat—when she stopped me. "John, I

216

want to tell you something. You're fluffing off these days. You're not truly working. What's happened is that you've got lazy."

Her eyes were blazing; I couldn't argue.

In my cell, hand under chin, I thought that she had kept this truth to herself all along. Through all her smiles—the Tennessee boy this, Tennessee that—she had known that I was lazy. For the past month or so I had been mainly copying up what I had written before, adding a little something here and there to give the illusion of newness. Spending time breaking the narrative down into chapters and then typing it up again pro-style on Eaton's Corrasable Bond made many a morning pass. What was frightening me was the thought that this monster, this load of typescript I had banged out and which Lowney had dubbed *The Thirst of Youth*, could be *completed*. Then, dear Jesus, it might be published. People would read it.

One item that clawed at the back of my mind was that— like a true Colony member—I'd have to compose the usual tribute to Lowney and Harry for the last page: "Grateful Thanks is Hereby Tendered." As Jim had done at the back of *Eternity*. Thank Lowney for the spiritual and material aid she had given; special thanks going to her for her editorial advice and encouragement in times of stress. Maybe I could dedicate the brute to her and get away without paying the tribute.

And what if I made money? Then there would be the problem of how to avoid building a house at the Colony.

And was I so proud of this creature that might fight its way to daylight? Much of it had come from deep recesses in me, was the truth as I saw it at twenty-three—but what was Lowney's handiwork? The Colony's? Mine? It didn't belong

217

to me alone. Nothing I had written had made me want to wake a friend at three o'clock in the morning and say, "Get a load of this, kid." Here I had a glut of Tom Wolfe-ian prose, and what I would have settled for was the knack for turning out pulp detective yarns that would have allowed me to travel the globe and call myself a writer.

And now—electric heaters going in our cells to ward off chilliness—old Mrs. Handy asked me where I planned to spend the winter. The thought of returning to the ground-floor room in her Victorian frame house, eating poached eggs in the kitchen where my brains had nearly been scrambled, made me gasp. And one evening in Lowney's bungalow, being given a Masters of the Far East tome and told to read it, I felt suddenly that same sense of imminent suffocation. Out of my mouth, unbidden, came, "Lowney, I cannot stay here this winter. I simply can't, no matter what."

"I wouldn't want you to," she said sweetly. And then these words sprung from her, seemingly unbidden: "You've done so much. You must be terribly tired. At times my heart goes out to you—to all of you boys locked up in this place. You sacrifice so much here, wanting to write. Do be gone this winter. Live, enjoy yourself—do whatever in the world you want to do. We'll keep in touch by letter, but you can always come to me—day or night—if you get in trouble. You don't even have to write to me if you don't feel like it. Just have a beautiful vacation. You've earned it."

I saw myself trotting to my cell, throwing my imitation-alligator bag in the back of my Plymouth, and speeding from the grounds. With a send-off like that, I wouldn't have any guilt in leaving. "Maybe in the morning I'll pack up and take off," I said.

"Take off? Oh, no, you're not. *Not until you finish your book!"*

Stated baldly like that, the terms for my parole, simplified matters. I'd just go ahead and finish the book. All I had to do was show my hero, Charley Henderson, a de-egoized guitar strummer, burning middle-class bridges behind him and taking the first step on the road to show biz, if not artistic, success. I'd outlined what was going to happen so often in avoiding writing it that I could almost use the outline itself. Charley had dropped out of college, had abandoned home and its ideas, and now all I had to do was show him playing for peanuts in a beer joint and have him discovered (à la Hollywood) by a shrewd agent who gleaned his potential. Not so hard. A few crisp scenes, leaving much blessedly to suggestion, should do it.

On a clear, crisp morning I rolled a clean yellow second into my machine, took a bite on a Lowney relative's apple, and put my hands on the keyboard. . . . Nothing. . . . Well, that happens. I stood and paced my cell, hearing sporadic gunfire from the machines down the line. Then I started to get back in the cockpit, but—like Gregory Peck in *Twelve O'Clock High,* paralyzed in trying to climb aboard his bomber for his final mission—I couldn't move. I felt a wet chill start at my forehead and spiral down my back; breaking out in a cold sweat is no misnomer, I thought, tucking that fact away for later fictional use. I went out in the sun by the drainage ditch to the lake, squatted, and threw pebbles into a clump of bushes. I tried so hard to think, in the grip of total mental constipation, that I fell over. "This is it," I told myself. "Get out of here. No matter what they say, get out of this place."

219

"Lowney, could I talk to you a second?" I said at her screen door.

"Why, of course. Come in," she said, in her sweetest of sweet voices. "Lean back in that chair. Relax awhile. Would you like to go into Terre Haute this afternoon?"

"Lowney—I . . . " and I saw her eyes grow large. She was looking at my hands. My hands were shaking as if in palsy. Violently and uncontrollably. They fascinated me, too.

"Johnny, I'm going to give you a drink. Anything you like. What'll it be? Scotch, bourbon, gin. I keep 'em all here for company."

"I'll take a martini."

A hawking throat clearing, shuffling feet, and Jim loomed in the doorway with his morning mug of coffee. "What's going on?"

"Jamie, fix this boy a martini. He can go back to his room and drink it. He needs it."

"Sure," he twanged, grinning, happy that a compliment had been paid to the power of his drink. "I'll make you a whole batch. What'd you like in it? Olive or lemon?"

I couldn't decide which. A simple choice like that, and it was beyond me.

"I'll give you a handful of both. You can make up your mind later."

I carried a fruit jar full of martinis, ice tinkling, into my room. Stretched out on my bunk, I drank from one of Jim's special martini cups, munching the olives after dipping them in the sharp, clear juice. And could I have finished the jar off so soon? Surely the ice had taken up tremendous room, given the illusion that more alcohol had been there than was. Standing, I felt a good warmth start at my stomach and billow out tenderly through my brain. The force of martinis was overrated, though; anybody could handle them. I knew exactly what I was doing, could observe myself clearly, going from cell to cell, shouting, "Type, you dirty caged animals. You poor pathetic beasts, you think you're writing the Great American Novel. Ha!"

Eyes perked up from typewriters, amused and amazed.

Even going up to Jim's silver trailer at ten-thirty that morning, the holy time of writing, I saw in fine detail precisely what I was doing. There he was, in a T-shirt, hunched over his machine, an unabridged Webster's to the side, the tableau enclosed in a soft glow from a lamp. The author of *From Here to Eternity* at work, putting down million-dollar words. "Jim, could I trouble you for another batch of martinis? I haven't felt a thing from the first one. Don't know why. Maybe you could use a larger-size fruit jar this time. Sorry to bother you like this, your writing and all. *Yipeeeee!*"

"Sure"—grinning delightedly. "I'll keep making 'em as long as you keep drinking 'em."

In my room I had worked myself through over three-quarters of a king-sized fruit jar when my clear-eyed vision left me, and four days and four nights went by in brief, unconnected flashes: Lowney frowning over me in a dim light, feeling my forehead, asking an unseen person if a doctor should be called; waking in darkness, my head sticky with puke; finding myself on the floor; throwing punches and being held down. A member (improbably destined to become Managing Editor of *Cosmopolitan* magazine) told me later: "We were all sitting down to lunch in the *ramada*—ears of corn I remember us having—when we heard singing coming from the barracks. It was one of those 1950, Lawrence Welk songs. Only you were using *fuck* and *shit* instead of the usual verbs. And did your voice carry! Somebody heard you on the highway. But Lowney pretended it wasn't happening, so we knew not to ask any questions. We did our chores and wrote right along as usual, ignoring your screams and the way your head sounded bouncing off the floor. We thought you were dying several times."

When I awoke, it was as if a new world had taken the place of the old and I was a baby taking my first steps. I held on to walls and groped my way for a long shower. In the *ramada*, waves of dizziness going through me, I got down half a cup of scalding black coffee. Comrades stepped up in turn to take brief looks at me, as if I were in a coffin. I saw wonder in their eyes, a little fear, and a new respect. I opened my mouth to speak, but only a strangled whisper came out. My God, I've been struck dumb. I got into my Plymouth—asking no one's permission, inviting no one else along—and drove to Terre Haute. Lowney had asked me if I wanted an afternoon off in the city, hadn't she? What if it had been four days ago? In my books that invitation still stood.

My first stop was a plain, old-fashioned grocery store where I bought two quarts of cold milk. Delicately, drinking it down in a slim trickle, I polished off both containers. I said a few words in the air, seeing how much of my voice I could bring back: "Good evening, ladies and gentlemen, so nice of you to come." Knowing now I could make myself understood, I drove to the whorehouse. I didn't know when I might be back this way again.

I chose a familiar face, the once-very-pretty woman with the unnaturally coal-black hair, the walking legendary suction pump. She had been among the troupe of girls my first visit there when I was a stranger in the nuances and protocol of an Al Capone-engineered establishment. While we were on the 'arf part of an 'arf 'n 'arf—my claw plugging her dyke

Dutchboy style because the puckered thing was looking me in the eye and I had to do something—we talked. Me in a hoarse whisper, her pausing between plunges. She would be discussing something in a normal, everyday voice, and then sink wetly down in a concert of licks and smacks and sucks that caused my eyeballs to roll back in my head.

"You still over at that farm with what's his name?"

"Yeah. Jones. We're writers."

"I know. Everybody says he wrote a dirty book and had a lot of swear words in it." Down like a butterfly with a little trill work that was especially pleasing, up like on a lollipop. My finger gave an encouraging flutter. "As soon as I can lay my hands on a copy, I'm going to read it. I want to see if it's as dirty as they say it is. I hope so."

"It's not dirty the way you think it might be, so save your money—*oh, baby, that's the stuff*.... It's a serious book, and the words and situations he uses are absolutely necessary for what he is writing about. He's not trying to titillate you. And he did a tremendous job, I'll tell you that. His book is strong enough and true enough to have changed a generation."

"You never know then. Fellow came in here the other day—big businessman in town, pillar of the community, I know for a fact—and we got to talking about Jones' book. I don't know, maybe I said something about you boys from the farm coming here, something, but we got off on the book. This man said it was the most perverted thing he'd ever tried to read, that he had burned it before his wife or teen-age daughter could get a peek at it."

"Yeah? You're kidding."

"No, I'm not. I know this type of guy, too, believe me. And guess what?"

"What?"

223

"While he was going on about how dirty and perverted this kind of book is, how booksellers that deal in 'em ought to be shot, he goes down on my pussy. And, sweetheart, I don't mean maybe. He eats that thing like he'd been starved for it for fifteen years. He licks it, smells it, damn near gets his big bald head in. I had to pry him loose finally and he was pretty close to passing out by then, that's how hungry for cunt he was."

"Yeah?" I'd sort of been drawn to her pucker myself a couple of times, what the hell, but figured if lip-kissing was off limits, then surely protocol wouldn't allow a buzz on the other region. "What happened?"

"I told him *he* was perverted." Down and up, and showed me her tongue. "Also, I charged him an extra five bucks. The house rule states that anyone who eats pussy has to pay an extra five dollars. You want it like this, or you want to get on top of me?"

*

From the whorehouse I went to the quiet and dimness of a movie theater, a picture starring Gary Cooper, and then I drove back to the Colony. The next morning, I drank a cup of Instant Maxwell House, ate two pieces of raisin-bread toast, and marched back to my cell. I rolled a yellow second in my machine and began typing without hesitation. I kept working straight for two and a half solid weeks—in the afternoons with no one's permission, into the night. Through a cold, a complaint from an abused prostate gland, and nightmares in which I awoke screaming, "Momma." Early one evening I typed the last word, plunked down the final period, and

224

walked immediately with a carton of typescript on Eaton Corrasable Bond to Lowney's bungalow. "Here it is," I said, handing it over and walking away.

I sat on the edge of my bunk, feeling nothing, staring at the floor, waiting for the first surge of happiness to hit me at the thought of the task all finished, the privations and agonies ended. Only to hear Lowney's scream in the night. "Johnny, come here. Come here this second." She half-threw, half-handed me the pile of manuscript. "This won't do. You've wrapped everything up too arbitrarily, too slickly. It happens in life that way, but it can't in fiction. You must leave the impression in fiction that everything happens by a Grand Design, that nothing happens by chance or due to fickleness. Go do this ending again."

I took the manuscript back to my cell, and began again. A week and a half later—it was so cold in my cell now that I wore two sweaters and kept the electric heater going constantly—I walked back to Lowney with a new version. I didn't allow myself the luxury of hope. . . .

"This could be better," she said, "but I think I'll let it go. I wish you had put in more about the sheriff, but it's too late for that now. It's done. It's finished. Well"—that enormous white smile breaking— "congratulations. I knew you could do it."

I was allowed to mail the manuscript of *The Thirst of Youth* to a New York agent. "Do you want us to put your carbon in a vault for safekeeping?" Lowney said. "We'll put it right alongside Jim's copy of *Eternity*. It'll be safe that way."

"No, no thanks, I would sort of like to hang on to it." I didn't want to leave anything behind that could possibly rope me back. Any rewrites I'd do in Timbuctoo. I said all my good-byes in one swoop, hurriedly, in the black of night.

225

"Take care of yourself and don't hitch up with an idiot woman," Lowney said. "We'll see you soon. Anytime. You can always come back."

"Be seeing you, buddy," Jim said. "Keep your pecker in your pants!"

On down the line, surprising Perc at some knitting, George with eyes glued to Willard Motley. Swift, embarrassed hand pumpings, glances that said, "Well, what do you know! The guy's going to escape after all and not over the wall either."

I slept for a few hours, flinging myself from the bunk while stars still shone in the sky, the earliest time I had ever arisen at the Colony. I got in my car—packed the night before with my few possessions—and was grateful to hear the battery kick over and the motor catch. I let the engine warm, looking over the calm dark lake, my teeth chattering from the cold. No sound came from the barrack cells because all doors were closed to the cool fall air. Lowney's tree-rimmed bungalow was dark and silent, and so was Jim's silver trailer. I glanced around in a full circle once, and then I drove onto the gravel by the *ramada* toward the outside.

The shell of Jim's new bachelor home rose in a pale grayish light from the harvest moon. I saw tools that had been dropped on the spot by the local carpenters when quitting time had sounded the previous afternoon, the cement bags partially covered by a tarpaulin, the wooden horses left standing for sawing. That crazy house was actually going to be completed—no doubt about it. And a curious statement I had heard from Jim not many days before surfaced in my mind: *"Boy, ain't all this something we can tell our children someday!" He* thought he was going to have children someday, really did, a regular family life—in the midst of this bar-

226

ricaded bachelor domain, the iron specter of Lowney T. Handy never more than an ax handle away. It would take more than dynamite ever to get him out.

Well, not me, O Lord, not me. I was escaping. Wonders and adventures lay waiting there outside. I would simply pick Love up where I had left it off in Tennessee. Now I was ready for life's sweets. I threw the gear in third, speeding past Jim's ghostly prison house, singing *Camptown Racetrack, doo-dah! Doo-dah!*

Off to:

Townfolk in Tennessee looking at me strangely when I said I was a writer, more strangely yet when I spouted off a Colony insight or aphorism. Finding the only job I could get was with a construction outfit twenty miles from home, starting time five A.M.; watching my mother come uncomplainingly but creakily and sleepy-eyed down the stairs to fix my breakfast. To be reported to the police as the suspicious character seen circling the block, time after time, where a certain couple lived. And then running into Juanita by chance, in life's fickle way, downtown, with nothing prepared and tongue-tied. She wore glasses, seemed to have put on weight. "Everything has a way of working out for the best," she said. "You had a dream. I hope you haven't lost it."

"But couldn't we just have a cup of coffee together? Talk together for just a moment?"

"Why, John, I'm married now. My husband is very jealous."

Getting a letter on classy stationery from the New York agent, saying he had thoroughly enjoyed my book, was optimistic that it could be sold, but warned that the market was bad—could have been sold in a minute a few years back, et cetera, et cetera. Such a well-written letter that I started copying certain parts of it for my own delivery. Henceforth, it became standard to close my letters with, "Best." The one thing that bothered me was not whether my book had a chance or not, but whether I should address my agent by his first name. Would that be presumptuous of me? I kept fretting about the sensibilities of this unseen, New York man, hoping I wasn't causing him too much trouble.

Lowney's letters embarrassed me: "THAT BOOK OF YOURS SHOULD BE SOLD NOW! Either that agent I latched onto for you shits, or he should get off the pot, as we say back in Kentucky. I CARRIED EIGHT MANUSCRIPTS WITH ME TO NEW YORK, and I come back with seven. They steal you blind up there if you aren't careful. Copy. I've seen it work wonders. We're all fine. Jim's in his new house." I hoped she hadn't upset my classy agent whom I was now calling by first name. He wrote—you could picture him chuckling—that he did appreciate Mrs. Handy's enthusiasm, but perhaps it carried her away into being overly optimistic about the market, which was bad, et cetera, et cetera. In any case, he understood.

Abandoning the misery of a five A.M. job and driving to L.A., the land, Colony legend had it, for easy, fly-by-night jobs and immediate pussy. Expecting starlets to be living next door in a lively boardinghouse, time set aside in the mornings for Colony-style composing.

The first night there I picked up a divorcée in tight clothing in the Avalon Ballroom, went to her place in the far reaches of Santa Monica, waited while she shed her tight clothing in an unseen room, and watched her reappear in the lacy black of Frederick's of Hollywood. "Don't get any ideas," she said. "I just changed to get more comfortable." Into *that?*

"Oh, baby," I said, Colony style, grabbing her, "let me fuck you till kingdom come."

"Leave these premises," she screamed. *"I can't stand that word!"*

Pumping gas in the shadow of M-G-M, my family believing from my letters that I'd snuck into the executive world of the fabled Western oil business and thanking God I'd given up the foolishness of trying to be a writer. Now actually seeing starlets enter a movie studio. Once I saw a devastating blonde being wheeled past the gates in a sparkling convertible driven by a bronzed stud in a blue polo shirt. My hands blackened with grease that wouldn't come off completely no matter how hard I scrubbed, keeping me from lighting strange women's cigarettes in bars; my dignity shot by having to run to the driver's side and blare, "Fill 'er up, sir?" I thought that if I could ever drive through those gray gates with that sort of blonde beside me, I'd be the happiest man on earth. (Ten years later to the day I *did* drive through those same gates in a convertible, a breathtaking blonde indeed beside me and—you guessed it—I was just as miserable and lonely. A new set of problems—more complex than those of a gas-station attendant—weighed on my shoulders. And few things are sadder than fantasies that come true ten years too late.)

Bearing down on one cylinder at all those jobs that presented themselves by chance—a taxi driver in Hollywood, a gambling shill in Nevada, a waiter at a fancy ski resort. After I'd broken my leg the third time out on skis, resuming my waiter's functions through the scientific advances of a walking cast, I wrote Lowney to say that I'd found the ultimate sport, the one that Jim could really kill himself in. And at nights coupling with the even-tempered cashier, who sat perched on a high stool through the day, on the floor of the dark and deserted restaurant. Grinding away with the purpose of a mole, under a table and awash wall-to-wall carpeting, at times the defective clean-up man almost catching us at it, his gently humming sweeper once nipping my plaster-encased foot at the prime, cascading moment. Was the essence of love's declaration destined to be consummated beneath tables, in backseats, on hillsides, and atop swaybacked beds with the bright lights on? Was making a mockery of it a way of not taking it seriously—allowing one to keep pure his higher Colony aspirations? *They want to trap you and bring you into a nest, Johnny! An Artist is not a Householder!* But who was writing, after coupling at night beneath tables and waking in the morning in a stinking male ski dorm?

Back to Tennessee to make a charade of the Colony routine. Rising early, having a cup of coffee in silence, and then going to my upstairs room to copy the Greats for a spell before springing into my own prose. I wrote a second novel, if you could call it that, much shorter than the Lowney-imposed one, with a filling-station setting, a scene that had tormented me. *Hate, envy, and malice are what spur a writer on! Use them!* That manuscript down the chute, another series of letters from the agent beginning on a "bad-market" note, and I lost heart.

In Washington, D.C., our nation's capital—where hope should start, but despair usually does, and where by chance I happened to be—I lost heart. I sold out to wear a suit through the day, have enough income so that I could take a girl to a movie, and to stop blushing when asked what I did for a living. Now it was, "I work for the Department of State." What could be more respectable? I got respectability along with a pernicious case of paranoia, until that day I walked into the office of a crew-cut man, my boss, who had aphorisms from George Washington and Benjamin Franklin all over his walls and said I couldn't take it any more. My correspondence with the New York agent had petered out through ennui on both parts, and now my manuscripts were not going between publishers like a shuttlecock but were at the bottom of a trunk, aging along with me.

And the car where it had all started—the Plymouth that had once gleamed and purred on the street, the bed for Juanita and me, the cross-country vehicle that had had its time for the distinctive scent of freshness—I sold for fifty dollars, and glad to get it, to a pimpled adolescent in Annandale, Va., who souped it up immediately and crushed head on into a tree.

The final bridge burned behind me—respectability—I landed carless in New York, where, lolling with Juanita on those dreamy spring nights, I had wanted to be—with her—in the first place. And then I started getting money for writing. After I'd really given up all hope, I started being paid for words I typed on paper, paid with checks that could be taken to a bank and exchanged for green notes that could in turn be exchanged for booze and other essentials. After I had been hired as an associate editor for a string of men's adventure magazines—a proud post—I had written one of my final letters to Lowney T. Handy. Throughout it all, the skiing accident, the accident of thinking I might make the grade as a career diplomat, she would whip back a six- to ten-page letter, single-spaced, every time I dropped her a line. I would slip a letter in the slot, and could count on a return answer being at whatever cramped space I called home almost by the time I got back. The adventure magazines featured on their wildly colored covers a lone bare-chested Yank, machine-gunning battalions of Nazis and Nips, a stiletto-heeled lady in black lace panties and bra conveniently but inexplicably at his side, a machine gun of her own frequently spurting away. I loved that job. "I was thinking of you just the other day. IT MUST BE INTUITION. About your brother, college, the fact that you got a BUM DEAL on your novel. You were voted down at Random House. One old man liked it, I forget his name; he edited Sinclair Lewis. (AND I KNOW I TOOK EIGHT MANUSCRIPTS TO NEW YORK and came back with seven. They stole one off me.) I had a stroke not long ago"—Lowney with a *stroke*, a health problem? Impossible—"and the doctors tell me not to write these long letters; it's going to kill me, but I must go on till someone takes my place. You say you are an editor now. YOU COULD BE DESTINED TO TAKE OVER FOR ME. Someone must. I've lost my best student, the first one I ever had. . . . LET HIM GO. . . . Your turning into an editor now could be destiny's way of saying YOU WILL TAKE OVER NOW. Think about it."

Back in touch, I grew nostalgic. I wanted to know what had happened to certain fondly remembered people from the Colony. I told her that I'd recently caught Norman Mailer's act in New York. Her answer, the final one, was the shortest I ever got from her. "Dearest Johnny: Your trouble as ALWAYS is living in the past. CHRIST SAID, 'Let the dead bury the dead.' I can't remember what Norman looks like, AND I'D NOT WANT TO BE CLOSER THAN TWO HUNDRED MILES TO HIM or anyone else you mention. Do you think I recall anyone who was ever in the camp? . . . Not a soul. If I had to give a remembered picture of James Jones to the cops, I sure as hell couldn't do it. That was another life. THE HANDY COLONY IS NO

232

MORE. I died. Now see if you can write. Love and kisses, L." I dropped the letter and let it lay, not putting it away until several months later.

I might have continued on forever as a men's-magazine editor if I'd learned to catch misspellings of *Wehrmacht* and Surigao Strait, unraveled the conundrum of red-hot blurb writing, and hadn't been offered outrageous sums to do articles for regular magazines, those with IKE and JFK and girls in puffing crotch bikinis on the covers. I never tried for them. An editor of a higher-paying magazine would read something in a lesser market, call me with an assignment, and I'd step up a rung on the ladder. That was how it was done. That simple. The Columbia School of Journalism was turning out hundreds of eager writers each year, all thirsting for the few assignments going out. Not to mention the other great universities of our land and their treadmills. And here I was, a Colony grad, now in a trench coat, hotfooting it around the globe like Richard Harding Davis to the beat of the news. "There's this quarterback the Jets just signed—Namuth, Namath, something like that. Follow him around. Go down to Birmingham with him. I hear he's still taking courses down there at the university. They're giving the guy four hundred thousand dollars—if you can believe it. It should be a story of some sort." And, "There's this kid named Sharon Tate. Philippe Halsman says she photographs better than any broad yet. She's hanging out in London now. Go over and follow her around. Then tag along when she's out in Hollywood. The angle will be how a beautiful piece of fluff breaks into the dream factory—or busts in the attempt—whichever. Have a ball, and make sure you turn in some kind of expense account. . . . "

And I heard about the Colony and those who had touched

it from the news, from the books they wrote, from letters. "You wouldn't believe the change in Lowney," Nelms had written. "She's turned almost completely white-headed and she's so gentle and liberal-minded at times that you can't believe it's her. It's almost as if she'd been defeated."

When *Some Came Running* came out, I got a copy. It said, in the blurb, that it might be the longest book ever published in America. I read here and there in it. The other Colony books—from an inherently diverse crowd—began to read alike, as if the same person had penned them. And thumbing the pages, I could picture scribbled on the margins: "Terrific!" "Beautiful, beautiful, keep it up!" Before I knew it, new writers had come to the Colony, had been initiated by nights in a tent, had sweated it all out, and had published *War and Peace*-length books with the standard tribute to Lowney at the end. There they were, intense young men I'd never met or heard quote the Masters of the Far East, staring like Jim from the back of book jackets.

And the news items that came abruptly, leaping from a casually opened paper or news magazine. James Jones marrying a woman from New York. James Jones living in New York. James Jones moving to Paris. A daughter born to the Joneses. And finally, so abruptly, scarcely a month after my last letter from her: Lowney T. Handy dies in Illinois. She had been in poor health, but it was unexpected. She was alone at the time.

But now, as I sped past Jim's shell of a house that gray dawn, I could not even have come close to predicting these events. (Could I have predicted the sight of Montgomery Clift coming up Third Avenue in his last days, a gaunt and broken old man? Could I have foreseen calling Jim one rainy night in Paris and thinking, from his reserved and cultivated

234

tone, that he must surely be the butler? Could I have imagined a Great Society leveling the whorehouses of Cherry Street, antiseptic high rises going up in their places? And would I have believed that Charley Hickerson, who had chosen the route of homebody and husband, would die in a freak accident before thirty by falling from a moving car?)

I was wrong about the wonders and adventures that lay outside. They were more—at times less—than I expected. (The elderly drunken woman in L.A. hitting me on the head with her purse as I tried in vain to find the mumbled address she gave me, knocking my Yellow Cab hat off, saying, "Ya goddam punk Okie shit, why don't you go back to where you came from?" And I was looking for starlets yet?) And, finally, I was wrong in thinking I was leaving the Colony.

For, as with Juanita, you do not leave anyone, or anyplace, by driving away. If they are strong enough, they live with you forever.

But at twenty-four, cutting down a paved street from the Colony that led to the highway, I leaned back in ecstasy and luxurious ease. *Free!*

> The Camptown ladies sing this song,
> Doo-dah! Doo-dah!

Yes, all of it out there waiting, waiting!

> I came down here with a
> pocket full of tin,
> doo-dah, doo-dah!
> I'm goin' back home with
> my hat caved in,
> Oh, doo-dah day!

ABOUT THE AUTHOR

John Bowers was raised and educated in Tennessee. A former cabdriver, gambling shill, construction laborer, and State Department Personnel Officer, he has published articles in *Playboy*, *Harper's*, *The Saturday Evening Post*, *New York*, and *Cosmopolitan*. Mr. Bowers lives in Greenwich Village in New York City.